"Dave Harvey encourage church leaders to embrace God's p... their weakness. He also reminds us that great joy comes along with the suffering as we care for the Lord's sheep. I counsel many discouraged pastors, and I am excited to be able to give them this resource, which will encourage them to continue to be vulnerable for Christ's sake and to endure."

Jim Newheiser, Professor of Christian Counseling and Pastoral Theology, Reformed Theological Seminary, Charlotte; executive director, The Institute for Biblical Counseling and Discipleship (IBCD)

"This book is balm and strength for leaders who love Christ's church and are feeling swamped by the suffering which their vocation as pastors entails. Dave Harvey opens his heart, sharing his long experience, and shows how leaders united to Christ will embody the gospel of Jesus's own dying and being made alive. A courageous book to bring strength in weakness."

Clive Bowsher, Provost, Union School of Theology, United Kingdom

"This book is for leaders, but if I'm being honest, it's a must-read for every believer today. Dave conducts a masterclass in his latest work, showing us that weakness is one of the most counterintuitive but essential aspects of our faith. With sincere honesty and humble vulnerability, Dave shows us that weakness is the way—the way to true flourishing in Christ."

Jonathan D. Holmes, Executive Director, Fieldstone Counseling; board member, the Christian Counseling and Educational Foundation (CCEF)

"With deep biblical insight and personal vulnerability, Dave Harvey presents an essential resource for leaders. In a day when many pastors and leaders are resigning, the call for biblical resilience is paramount. This book provides the often-overlooked secret to ministry resilience—discovering God's power through our weakness. I enthusiastically recommend this book, and I pray its core message will be received with joy and applied with faith."

Robbie Symons, Lead Pastor of Preaching and Vision, Hope Bible Church Oakville, Ontario

"Dave Harvey's wisdom, forged through suffering, makes this an essential read for every pastor and ministry leader. Don't hesitate—pick it up! You won't regret it. You'll be as blessed as if you were sitting with him, hearing him open his heart and urge you to stand firm no matter what you're facing."

Felix Cabrera, Founder, Endos Network

"This is a book filled with heartbreak and hope, chronicling the life of a man who has not only walked with the

Lord during seasons of brokenness and heartache, but has been carried by him through the darkest valleys. Dave reminds us through story and Scripture that our weakness is the means by which God produces wholeness in us. A phenomenal piece of work that will help and encourage many."

Ronnie Martin, Director of Leader Care and Renewal, Harbor Network; pastor-in-residence, Redeemer Church, Bloomington, Indiana

"It has been one of the most difficult lessons I have ever had to learn, that God delights to use weak people. God does not use weak people by first making them strong, but by keeping them weak. Why? Because their weakness provides the greatest opportunity for God to display his power. This is the clay pot conspiracy that Dave Harvey unveils in this powerful, necessary book. I highly recommend you read it."

Tim Challies, Author of *Seasons of Sorrow*

"Dave Harvey helps us all with the timely reminder that when we acknowledge our dependence upon God, we find that weakness is an advantage!"

Alistair Begg, Senior Pastor, Parkside Church; Bible teacher, Truth For Life

"I'm grateful for Dave Harvey's *The Clay Pot Conspiracy* because of how he points leaders to the true gospel where, like Jesus, we minister out of suffering. I pray you'll read this book and join the conspiracy of Christlike leadership it lovingly outlines."

Jared C. Wilson, Assistant Professor of Pastoral Ministry, Midwestern Seminary; pastor for preaching, Liberty Baptist Church; author of *Lest We Drift*

"Dave has suffered family and ministerial heartbreak—trials that can wreck a person's faith. Yet, all Dave can talk about is Jesus. With the loveliness of Jesus set before us, Dave counsels us with wisdom, grace, clear talk, honest weakness, and the kind of humor that mends a soul. Dear leader, Jesus has met Dave in the broken places. Dave testifies that Jesus can meet us there too."

Zack Eswine, Lead Pastor, Riverside Church; author of *The Imperfect Pastor*

"With biblical insight and raw personal stories, Dave Harvey reminds us that the steep road of sorrow isn't an aberration but a promised part of the journey toward glory. Drawing especially from the apostle Paul, he shows how our frailties are not barriers to ministry but the very means by which God displays his goodness and love. A powerful book forged through sorrow and joy."

Trevin Wax, Vice President of Resources and Marketing, North American Mission Board; author of *The Thrill of Orthodoxy, Rethink Your Self,* and *Gospel Centered Teaching*

THE CLAY POT CONSPIRACY

GOD'S PLAN TO USE WEAKNESS IN LEADERS

By Dave Harvey

newgrowthpress.com

New Growth Press, Greensboro, NC 27401
newgrowthpress.com
Copyright © 2025 by Dave Harvey

All rights reserved. No part of this publication may be reproduced, stored in a retrieval system, or transmitted in any form by any means, electronic, mechanical, photocopy, recording, or otherwise, without the prior permission of the publisher, except as provided by USA copyright law.

Unless otherwise noted, all Scripture quotations are taken from The ESV® Bible (The Holy Bible, English Standard Version®). ESV® Text Edition: 2016. Copyright © 2001 by Crossway, a publishing ministry of Good News Publishers. The ESV® text has been reproduced in cooperation with and by permission of Good News Publishers. Unauthorized reproduction of this publication is prohibited. All rights reserved. Used by permission.

Scripture quotations marked NASB are taken from New American Standard Bible®, Copyright © 1960, 1971, 1977, 1995, 2020 by The Lockman Foundation. All rights reserved. Used by permission.

Scripture quotations marked NIV are taken from THE HOLY BIBLE, NEW INTERNATIONAL VERSION®, NIV® Copyright © 1973, 1978, 1984, 2011 by Biblica, Inc.® Used by permission. All rights reserved worldwide.

Scripture quotations marked LSB are taken from The Legacy Standard Bible® (LSB®), Copyright © 2021 by the Lockman Foundation. Used by permission. All rights reserved. Managed in partnership with Three Sixteen Publishing, Inc. 316publishing.com.

Cover Design: Pete Garceau
Interior Typesetting and Ebook: Lisa Parnell, lparnellbookservices.com

ISBN: 978-1-64507-540-0 (paperback)
ISBN: 978-1-64507-541-7 (ebook)

Library of Congress Cataloging-in-Publication Data on file

Printed in Colombia

29 28 27 26 25   1 2 3 4 5

For Pete

*My clay pot mate who has spent
decades of friendship embodying the conspiracy
and calling me to do the same.*

CONTENTS

FOREWORD	xi
INTRODUCTION	1
WONDER #1: STORE TREASURE IN CLAY	9
WONDER #2: MAKE DEATH PRODUCE LIFE	33
WONDER #3: LET REPENTANCE STOKE RESILIENCE	57
WONDER #4: LEARN LOVE WHEN THE CHURCH WOUNDS YOU	75
WONDER #5: REMEMBER GOD USES ENEMIES TO ENLARGE YOUR SOUL	97
WONDER #6: BUILD STRONG TEAMS THROUGH WEAK LEADERS	121
WONDER #7: RUN TOGETHER TO FINISH WELL	143
EPILOGUE	167
ACKNOWLEDGMENTS	171
ENDNOTES	173

FOREWORD

Deep heartache is not an unfortunate accident some ministry leaders stumble into while the rest of us look on sympathetically. Deep heartache is the path that all true ministry leadership takes.

We all know this, at one level. We see it everywhere in Scripture—in Moses's leadership, in David's psalms of lament, in Christ's teaching, in the weakness celebrated in 2 Corinthians, in the pastoral charges of 1 and 2 Timothy.

But it is another thing to be plunged into this truth personally, abruptly, surprisingly, painfully. The unique ministry of this book by my friend Dave Harvey is that it takes us into the heartaches of New Testament ministry under the guidance of someone who knows what he is talking about from the inside. Dave does not write about the anguish of pastoral work in a clinical, detached way. With redemptive transparency, Dave shares some of his own weaknesses and sufferings. As we less experienced ministry leaders read, we find ourselves thinking: *This man gets me. He's been down the road I'm walking. I thought my ministry travails were unusual. They're not. And not only are they normal, they're needed.*

This pain is not an optional ingredient to gospel ministry—it is a key ingredient. And it is a privilege to share just a bit in the sufferings of Christ. And we in ministry deeply accept the path that the Lord has laid for us, knowing that in his own way and in his own time, God will flip each little experience of death into a mighty permanent resurrection. That's what God is like. It's the path his own Son walked, and we are united to him.

In the meantime, we embrace our deep and unique weaknesses. They are not a problem; they are a strategy. They are the strange ingredient to God's own divine power quietly emerging in our ministry and leadership.

Dave Harvey writes to us as a friend, a brother, a counselor. This book is biblical, and therefore can be trusted. But this book can be trusted for another reason: Dave reflects on ministry with both scars and laughter. I trust a man who is standing tall with both after forty years of pastoring. The cynical pastor has scars, but no laughter. The frothy pastor has laughter, but no scars.

FOREWORD

Dave has both acute pain in his life and a joyful gleam in his eye. But joy is the major chord. How could it be otherwise? Dave follows in the footsteps of an apostle who was "sorrowful, yet always rejoicing" (2 Corinthians 6:10); the apostle who tells us to rejoice always (Philippians 4:4) just a few sentences after letting us know he is crying while writing (Philippians 3:18).

So I thank Dave for offering this book and its vital truths to the rest of us. For the message of this book is key to lasting in Christian leadership—and not just lasting, but rejoicing to the very end.

Dane Ortlund

INTRODUCTION

This morning, according to the calendar, is a new year. I hope so. Last year was a hard year. The caboose to a long, hard decade. I listened for our grandson, who sleeps like he's training for the Olympics. Our little slumber-lord. Four years ago on this very day, I discovered our youngest adult daughter was pregnant. She was never able to raise her son. Several years ago, at the age of sixty, my wife and I were given custody and became caregivers.

I took a deep breath. *Man*, I thought, *I really need a new year! Something with more wins. A factory-delivered, field-tested string of months that arrive with a little sparkle. Maybe even a warranty.* A cloud of gloom rose casting a shadow across my soul. My emotions missed the brake and went spiraling toward the pit. I knew this pit well. *"Hello darkness, my old friend . . ."* Paul Simon had been there too.

The tears came slowly. Shoot, I knew it. When I sleep less, I weep more. Or maybe I weep more because I sleep less. Who knows? After four decades in ministry, the whole sleep thing still eludes me. The pit does not.

WEEPING ALONE

I weep a lot these days. It's strange, but my tear ducts only work when I'm alone. Maybe it's a guy thing. Maybe it's because I want to control people's perception of me. Or maybe it's because I come from a long line of non-criers. Who knows? But when no one is around, I let the tears flow. It happens a lot, but it no longer scares me. Not anymore. The Bible has helped me to anticipate it. God has shown me his power through it. That's really important. We will come back to that thought many times in this book.

Last year was a hard year. I've had worse, but last year made the short list of "the worst of times." The loss of my mom, leadership loneliness, relational conflict, ministry betrayal, unrelenting fatigue, shame from the past, double-pneumonia for a couple of months, the feeling that ministry is filled with feckless effort. *Wow, some days I can't even remember the names of my grandkids, but that list rolled right off the tongue.*

What a depressing start to the new year.

Do you ever feel this way? You know, where the past is like a magnet growing stronger with age. When I was a younger leader, even into my early fifties, I was very forward looking. But the older I get, the greater the magnetic pull toward the past.

Reflecting back, the tears flowed more freely. I wept over pain and loss. I wept for the disconnect I often feel between how life should be and how it is. I wept over my weakness. The impact of my weakness and the ground war it wins each year. At my age, it feels like limitations lurk behind every corner waiting to mug me; a thief swiping some asset I used to possess. Memory, stamina, resilience are all stolen away by time and trouble.

A strong breeze blew; that's when I heard it.

OF CHIMES AND WONDERS

A set of wind chimes hangs on a tree in our yard. Five chimes dangle, like flutes suspended in space. Down the center runs a wooden ball attached to a fishing line. It hangs between the chimes. When the wind blows, the ball swings, and the chimes sing. A solid breeze creates a symphony of bells banging together, tolling for my attention.

I stopped ruminating to listen. The sound is distinct. Inviting. Beautiful and timely. Surprisingly *haunting*.

As the wind grew, the chimes soared with sound. Glancing over, a sunrise crested the hill and shafts of light beamed upon the musical mobile. Chimes swung back and forth like the pendulum on a clock, catching the sunbeams as they rocked eastward before they swayed back into the shadows. Morning broke as the chimes rocked from darkness to light, swinging between shadow and sun, clanging as it moved between blackness and beauty.

I closed my eyes and listened. That's when I noticed it. The chimes pitched wildly back and forth, yet the music remained unchanged. Strong. Resonant. Consistent. I felt summoned to listen.

I can't remember the last time I felt like an experience formed a metaphor for my life as a leader. But in that moment—as the winds of the new year were blowing—I sensed the chimes were an invitation from God. A reminder that my story was not unique; my pain, not uncommon; my tears, not unexpected. I remembered something it took me years to learn. My weakness was part of God's plot. His fruit-bearing plan. The hard, yet wonderful vehicle through which his power would flow.

Wiping my eyes, I thought about the new year. The winds will blow strong through ministry this year, I can already see that. Feel it. And the chimes of my aging body may swing wildly between shadow and sunlight.

INTRODUCTION

But sitting there, I realized that absent the wind and the turbulence of swinging, the chimes hang silent. There is no music. What a wonder that is!

GOD WANTS US TO CHIME FOR HIS GLORY

Be it good or bad times, weakness or strength, prosperity or adversity, God wants my life to chime for his glory. It's why he calls us to lead. But God has an unusual way of producing the music. A secret way. A mysterious and wondrously covert plan he uses for extracting his glory from the life of leaders.

> *Leadership was never about exalting our strengths. God's plan was always to deliver his strength through our weaknesses.*

It's a kind of incongruity that uncovers a conspiracy. I call it the *clay pot conspiracy*.

It's a simple equation:

Our Weakness + God's Power = Resilient Ministry

We'll unpack this equation by looking at seven surprising wonders, but for now let me say that the leader can neither manipulate nor escape God's counterintuitive plan. Nor would you ever want too.

You see, gospel ministry carries a clause. Suffering and sadness? Trauma? Fatigue and feebleness? You bet! It's all embedded in the call and part of the plan. You can't avoid it. It finds you. Then it transforms you and positions you for power. It's all part of the conspiracy.

God is not content to make us merely conversant about the gospel. Biblical leadership is a call to embody it. And the leader's capacity to persevere is connected to their understanding of that glorious, empowering reality.

No leader knows the baseline of suffering drawn for him by the hand of Providence. He can only know it is designed to uncover the conspiracy. Your story will be different from mine. But the goal will be the same. To draw back the curtain on God's plan to help you embody the gospel. If you enlisted in service of the gospel, you too will be caught up in this glorious wonder.

WILL YOU JOIN ME?

Seeing the chimes swing away from the sun, I was reminded of God's plan. It inspired me. Faith infused my

INTRODUCTION

soul as I remembered passages packed tight with promises. My tears evaporated. Learning how God works, sometimes surreptitiously, to ensure leaders understand and embody the gospel will change your life. It changes how you think about ministry and gives you a new arsenal of faith for endurance. Connecting the dots to how God's conspiracy helps us to last in ministry is going to transform how you move toward the future.

Our call is to make gospel music. Even as we swing between valleys and mountains, and shadows and sunlight. That's still our call. We are part of the clay pot conspiracy. And the more you see the brilliance and beauty of this plan, the more your journey in ministry makes sense. Your ministry is the instrument. The wind and the swings make the music. Gospel music.

Are you curious? Let's try this: Let's start an adventure together; let's explore the details and delights of God's clay pot conspiracy. You probably need it now more than ever. I know I do. Take the next step by looking deeper into the details behind the conspiracy. See you in chapter 1!

Wonder #1
STORE TREASURE IN CLAY

In 1947, a young Bedouin shepherd was herding his flock on a hill near the Dead Sea. Since sheep are prone to wander, one little lamb ambled away. The shepherd set out on a search that led him to a dark cave tucked away on the hillside of the northwestern ridge.

The young shepherd crept toward the cave mouth and peered inside. The genetic coding of every teenage boy determined what happened next. Yep, the shepherd boy found a rock and chucked it into the darkness. What he heard next astonished him. Something shattered. Crawling through the entrance, the intrepid shepherd came face-to-face with an archaeological wonder.

The boy found a row of enormous clay pots, larger than him—each one sealed shut. Popping one lid, he uncovered ancient scrolls inside—some wrapped in linen, others blackened to the point of being unreadable. Little did the shepherd know that he would be immortalized as the guy who discovered the Dead Sea Scrolls.

A treasure of incomprehensible value. Stored in clay pots.

CORINTHIAN CRITICISM

Make no mistake, leadership is hard. Maybe you're reading this and thinking, "I left Planet *Hard* a while back. I'm rocketing toward the moons of *Brutal*!" Yes, ministry can be brutal. But the depth of difficulty is often connected to the way it violates our expectations. *This is NOT what I expected!* We signed on for a cruise only to discover we have boarded a battleship. We came aboard assuming God recruited us to display our strengths. But the good ship *Ministry* sails in a different direction. A truly unexpected, covert bearing.

Weakness, that's our heading.

The journey toward ministry maturity and fruitfulness fixes us on a course toward weakness. In a fallen world, the most fruitful and durable ministry is always packaged up with—and revealed in—weak and broken vessels. Listen to how the apostle Paul describes it:

We have this treasure in jars of clay, to show that the surpassing power belongs to God and not to us. We are afflicted in every way, but not crushed; perplexed, but not driven to despair; persecuted, but not forsaken; struck down, but not destroyed; always carrying in the body the death of Jesus, so that the life of Jesus may also be manifested in our bodies. For we who live are always being given over to death for Jesus' sake, so that the life of Jesus may also be manifested in our mortal flesh. So death is at work in us, but life in you. (2 Corinthians 4:7–12)

Why is Paul portraying gospel ministry in such a confounding way? In Corinth there was a party opposed to Paul. Their mission was to tear people away from Paul's leadership, and to win the Corinthian believers over to their version of leadership success. Their strategy for achieving this was to attack and discredit Paul. "There can be no doubt," says Murray Harris, "that the primary aim of Paul's adversaries was to undermine and so destroy Paul's apostolic authority. What they taught was calculated to bring about Paul's downfall, at least in Corinth, and to establish their own credentials as authentic servants of Christ.[1]

It's an old-but-effective playbook. Strike the shepherd, the sheep scatter, and then wolves replace the shepherd and roast the sheep.

WHAT MAKES A LEADER ATTRACTIVE?

Paul's opponents despised weakness. They believed leadership meant putting on a show for others. They boasted in "face," not in heart, and they were trying to fool the Corinthians into believing that it was their outward appearance that mattered most (2 Corinthians 5:12). "Appearance counted for everything, as it often does today," says commentator Mark Seifrid. "One wonders how Paul would have fit into today's social media culture. At this point, there were few in Corinth who "liked" his message, and fewer still who were willing to "friend" him.[2]

Have you ever felt like there are things about you that make you less appealing as a leader? Gifts and graces you see in others and wish you possessed? Maybe it's the way you speak—you lack wit, charisma, too often your brain can't locate your tongue and you stumble to find words. Perhaps it's the way you look—a scar, a defect, your size, any other noticeable physical condition. Paul can relate. His appearance was . . . well, let's just say it gave the opposition party a lot to work with.

Tradition has it that Paul was unattractive. Many have observed that he suffered from an eye condition. That's why, when writing about the Galatian church's love for him, Paul says, "I can testify that, if you could have done so, you would have torn out your eyes and given them to me" (Galatians 4:15 NIV). Paul wasn't only weak in appearance; he sometimes came across as unskilled in his speech (2 Corinthians 10:10). He also carried no letters of commendation (2 Corinthians 3:1; 10:13–14)—the primary way back then of displaying street cred. From his antagonists' point of view, Paul was too plain. Too contemptible. Too *weak.*

We get it. It's how the world works. Nobody celebrates flunked tests or failed start-ups. You never find sports teams named after weakness. Imagine—"The Los Angeles Lambs are still 0–6 on the season." We can't imagine it because it would never happen.

At best, weakness is pitied. At worst, it's despised. Maybe you're living under that cloud right now, feeling friendless and feckless. Perhaps you're looking for a way to move forward. Check out what Paul does.

WEAKNESS—THE CORE LEADERSHIP CREDENTIAL

Paul counters with a decidedly unconventional defense. To the charge that he's insufficient, Paul says, "Guilty."

To the charge that he's an unrefined orator, Paul repeats, "Guilty." To the charge that he's weak, Paul asserts, "Guilty!" Paul flips the script on his detractors by saying, "You think my weakness disqualifies me. *But it's actually my core credential.*"

You see, Paul discovered a secret: His weakness was an opportunity for God's power. He learned that when weakness meets God's grace, strength abounds. It's what I like to call the *clay pot conspiracy*.

Although the word *conspiracy* has dark overtones and is frequently politicized, I think it accurately conveys the essence behind God's hidden agenda. After all, the conspiracy is not aimed at us. God coordinated a covert plan to sabotage an enemy who manipulates human power and strength. It's a magnificent plot where God recalibrates our metrics of success from human potency to Godward dependence. It's a secret design to humble the proud, abolish boasting, and establish the ground for our longevity.

Here is the simple formula for the clay pot conspiracy.

Our Weakness + God's Power = Resilient Ministry[3]

Slow down and roll this over in your mind for a moment. The vulnerability and frailty you are feeling right now are not a punishment; they are not a consequence of your narrow gifts or poor performance. That's what we often think, isn't it? I know I do. Each month I beat back some form of condemnation around poor performances or low-fruit places in ministry.

But then something happens. Through the incomparable power of God's living and active Word, I remember God's clay pot conspiracy. As I have studied 2 Corinthians along with other Bible passages, I've discovered seven different "wonders." These wonders point to the remarkable and mysterious ways God reanimates weakness for our good and his glory. Together they form God's blueprint for leadership longevity. I use the word "longevity" intentionally, because one of the clear aims behind this whole passage is to help leaders not "lose heart" (2 Corinthians 4:1, 16). God loves longevity. He wants leaders who last.

The wonders we are going to uncover are surprising because God's clandestine plan does not fit neatly within our categories for successful ministry metrics. There is little appeal to what we would naturally want or expect from leadership in this conspiracy. It takes time to see it and to hear it.

The wonders do not make us softer saints or less courageous leaders. This book is all about how God instills strength, boldness, power, and resilience in those he has called to be leaders. But let's be honest, this is counterintuitive. We don't expect to grow stronger by becoming broken, to experience power by becoming weak, or for God's plan for our leadership longevity to be so packed with paradox.

I was like that. But that was before God uncovered the first wonder within his conspiracy.

THE WONDER: STORE TREASURE IN CLAY

Here's how Paul describes this wonder: "We have this treasure in jars of clay, to show that the surpassing power belongs to God and not to us" (2 Corinthians 4:7).

What is the treasure Paul is talking about here? What does the pronoun "this" in "*this* treasure" refer to? To answer that question, we need to go back and look at the first six verses of the chapter. You can trace the antecedent of "this" back to verse 1 where Paul talks about the ministry he's been given through God's mercy. You see it again in verse 6 where he says that his ministry is to share the light of the knowledge of the glory of God to all peoples.

Paul's treasure is his gospel ministry. Paul is speaking first about the amazing worth of the incomparable Christ, the priceless message about the Savior who left the glory of heaven and died to save sinners. But the treasure for Paul is both the glorious news of Christ's completed work and *the ministry* of the gospel of the glory of God. Think of it like this:

Message + Ministry = Treasure

Gospel ministry is a privilege all Christian leaders share with Paul. It is a privilege entrusted to us when we enter ministry as leaders in the local church, Christian ministry, or the mission field. Regardless of the size of the ministry or the leadership role we occupy, we share the glorious honor of proclaiming the gospel of Jesus Christ, seeing the light of God's glory go forward through the finished work of Jesus. This is God's treasure.

But at the heart of this passage rests a stunning contrast. This incomprehensible treasure is stored in fragile jars of clay.

Clay jars had a range of uses. In 2 Timothy 2:20, Paul writes, "In a large house there are articles not only of gold and silver, but also of wood and clay; some are for special purposes and some for common use" (NIV). The 2 Corinthians 4 reference was not, however, the classy, upscale container. No, actually, think: jars you could find in a dollar store. These were the common-use pots in everyone's home. They were the containers where you stored things, and they were sometimes, well, let's just come out with it—the chamber pots!

The clay referred to here, is little more than baked dirt. Clay pots were for common use. Think about that. If you put it in today's language, clay pots are like those disposable rubber gloves in the hospital, or the foam coffee cups littered on the lawn after a church picnic. Paul uses the metaphor of the clay pot to convey something common, fragile, powerless, even breakable.

Paul is saying that he *is* a clay pot—an ordinary, brittle container. That's me too. And actually, you're a clay pot in this kitchen as well!

Just to be crystal clear, Paul isn't downgrading our worth, value, or dignity in this passage. As fragile as we may feel, the Bible tells us that we are made in God's image (Genesis 1:27) and he loves us with an everlasting love (Jeremiah 31:3). One of the loudest statements God can make about our value is that he has authorized us to carry his treasure.

Leader, God is talking to you. You have something of infinite value stored in your ministry, your body, your life, your clay pot. You are the receptacle; you are the earthen vessel in which the treasure of the gospel rests. Being like a clay pot can mean we are either fragile or disposal (or both), but each idea points to one common ingredient: the clay pot is a metaphor for weakness—our weakness.

THE WEALTH OF WEAKNESS

When I was seven years old, my brother—such a nutcase, my brother—called me over to the gravel parking lot across from our house. "Dave," he said. "Come here. I want to show you something." In his hand was a gold nugget—at least what looked like a gold nugget; I didn't yet see the gold spray-paint cans littered on the ground around his feet.

"Whoa! Where did you get that?" I said.

"Right here, man!" he said, as his arms spread wide. "And they're sprinkled all over the parking lot. It's filled with gold!"

I stood astounded. But my brother was just getting started. "And guess what? *I bought the whole lot!*"

Then he stepped forward. "And since I'm your brother, here's the first piece of gold from my new lot." He reached over and set the spray-painted piece of gravel in my sweaty hand. When I close my eyes, I can still remember the sensation of awe as I palmed this priceless mineral that had transformed me into a wildly wealthy kid.

Feeling now the burden of spontaneous wealth, I knew my gold needed to be secured. So I ran home, rushed upstairs, and grabbed a shoe box. I put my gold nugget in the middle of the shoe box, and I stuffed newspaper all around it. Then I wrapped it in duct tape (because we all know that duct tape is impregnable to burglars). The box then went into the bottom drawer of my dresser (because no criminal would *ever* think of going into the bottom drawer!). Even at seven, I knew that my treasure should be in the safest place I could find.

But God's strategy is different. God stores his treasure in something common and breakable. We think our battle with anxiety makes us less effective to lead. We assume our physical illness or prodigal child means the end of usefulness for God. We look in the mirror and walk away with a catalog of defects. To us, our weaknesses mean that we are less-than—less than worthy, less than useful, less than acceptable.

But beneath our pain there is a plan—it's the first wonder in the clay pot conspiracy. God is working to make your life shine in ways you never imagined. How? God stores his treasure in clay *to show that the surpassing power belongs to him and not to us* (2 Corinthians 4:7).

We are not always strong. We are human and frail. And the only way to experience God's surpassing power is to own our weakness and behold how God reanimates it for our good and his glory.

God stores his treasure in jars of clay. Can you own it?

THE WAY OF WEAKNESS

Owning starts with knowing. So let's begin to know the way of weakness by unwinding the meaning wrapped around the metaphor. What does weakness truly mean?

Weakness can be a general way to talk about the comprehensive human condition. We are imperfect, perishable, and fragile. It spills out every day. The use of "weakness" here is singular—a sweeping reference to the frailty and fallenness corrupting the occupants of a broken world. Yet the clay pot metaphor supplies more clarity, nuance, and detail to the idea of weakness.

To begin, weakness reveals our inadequacy. "For what is weakness?" asks J. I. Packer. "The idea from first to last is of *inadequacy*" (emphasis mine).[4] The first inkling that we are inadequate typically happens around conversion. Think back to those days, long before you were a leader. Do you remember how you became convinced that you were inadequate to save yourself? Effort and energy never moved the needle. You were trapped within the boundaries of your inability. But your substitutionary Savior came and swapped out your inadequacy for his adequacy. Christ's sufficiency resolved your insufficiency. That's where this whole journey started—with your complete and utter inadequacy.

But leadership arrived and something happened.

Inadequacy receded into the background. Gifts were identified. We assumed roles that played to our talents. Our strengths were affirmed and celebrated. Our service and performance generated respect and credibility. It wasn't easy, but we became adequate and able—a vessel that sparkled with significance. This seemed good and felt good. We wanted to look strong. We *needed* to look strong.

But it didn't last. Suffering made a surprise visit. Unexpected betrayal occurred. Deep disappointments landed. We are still sinners. We discover detractors. Detractors discover us. Demonic discouragement visits. Church leadership is nothing like what we expected. The balloon of our own strength, once so energizing and elevating, gets punctured. We stare into a mirror that reflects more and more weakness.

INADEQUACY: THE STAGE FOR POWER

Cheer up! Looking polished was never the point. "We have this treasure in jars of clay, to show that the surpassing power belongs to God and not to us." Inadequacy sets the stage to display something far more glorious than our strength. It's about God's power, not ours. It's about God's grace, not our grit. Whether you know it or not, a life where weakness reveals dependence upon God has always been the point of your call to leadership. D. A. Carson explains it like this: "God's strength is made perfect in weakness: it reaches its fullest measure and most powerful forms when issued in response to weakness. The greater the Christian's weakness, the greater the grace poured out."[5]

Let's do a check-up: Do people walk away from your leadership thinking more about you than God? Who is most magnified in your leadership? If I'm being honest, the answer to that question is, too often, me. I want people to see me through my strengths. I want the surpassing power ascribed to me—a clay-less composite of Dave.

Last year I got to thinking: *What might it look like for me to highlight the clay pot that is behind my ministry?* So I tried it. I was asked to supply a bio for a board where I served. This is what I wrote:

I'm not particularly imaginative or some kind of big change-agent. I have a remarkable wife, but we've experienced some challenges as parents. I've lost about 200 lbs. over the last twenty years, primarily by gaining and losing the same ten pounds. I like praise too much and wish I used my time better because I want to read much more than I do. Ministry over the decades has delivered incredible and undeserved joys, not to mention unimaginable sorrow. Whatever bitter taste there may be has made Christ sweet!

One small step for clay-kind.

We leaders are a funny lot. Each day our clay goes on full display. We skip appointments, manage disappointments, miss exit ramps, oversleep, misplace car keys, forget our phones, drop glasses, get irritated, become impatient, say things we shouldn't. Just a few sleepless nights can shatter us. We arrive into the world needy and, if we grow old, we plumb deeper into weakness before departure. Yet we often live in clay-denial, posing as the Creator even while we desperately prop up (or push down) our creatureliness.

On some level within us, the truth of our inadequacy is inescapable. To admit we are clay helps us to see through the scaffolding of strength we have erected to disguise our clay pot. But it's a relief when our inability comes into sharper focus. Acknowledging it puts us on the path toward power. God knows we're messy and weak. Do we know it? Can we own it?

WEAKNESS MEANS VULNERABILITY

What else do we need to know about weakness? It's important to know that weakness means *vulnerability*. Vulnerability is the risk imposed by our inadequacy. It's the powerlessness and exposure we accept when leading as a clay pot in a fallen world.

George Whitefield was undoubtedly a flawed vessel in God's service.[6] Yet he possessed a vision of ministry that embraced the risk of his inadequacy. Whitefield had a large network of churches in England when he felt called to preach for an extended period in the United States. To maintain his ministry, Whitefield arranged for a younger leader to manage the churches while he was gone. But the leader subverted Whitefield, shifting doctrines, co-opting affections, and winning people over to himself.

Whitefield returned to a ministry maelstrom of sabotage and betrayal. He became convinced it would be too divisive to fight for the church movement he started. He walked away and just started over. He took the hit. Maybe a more discerning eye would have detected the vulnerability or sniffed out this leader's corrupted ambitions before leaving. But Whitefield made a choice. By deciding to travel to the States, he opened himself up to significant loss. Much of his ministry was hijacked.

But Whitefield knew that risk and loss came with the call. His unusual gifts did not exempt him from exposure. Whitefield did not play the victim, demonize the leader, or contend for his place. He sought the strength that comes from weakness. Whitefield's loss became a way to display a surpassing power that belongs to God alone; to know Christ in the fellowship of suffering (Philippians 3:10). He later said, "It is good for me that I have been supplanted, despised, censured, maligned, judged by and separated from my nearest dearest friends. By this I have found the faithfulness of Him who is the friend of friends . . . and to be content that He to whom all hearts are open . . . now sees . . . the uprightness of my intentions to all mankind."[7]

Risk is the cost of making decisions without the luxury of omniscience. Whitefield could not see, nor could he fully calculate, the impact of his decision to travel. His inadequacy made him vulnerable to betrayal. God used this vulnerability for great good. The latter fruit of his ministry was greater than the former. But that did not exempt Whitefield from the emotional pain of leading as a clay pot. When the clay pot risked vulnerability, glory shone through.

To lead means we must bear risks. Each risk we take makes us vulnerable to others who don't understand or appreciate our actions. They may have their own agenda. We may have additional (and more accurate) information we are unable to share. In a climate where full access to all information by all people is seen as a constitutional right, being more principled will make you more vulnerable. True leadership means we carry some burdens so that others don't have to.

Leaders bear burdens so others can walk without the weight. But it strains the clay pot. Leaders become weaker. We learn to say with David, "As for me, I am poor and needy, but the Lord takes thought for me" (Psalm 40:17a).

Sometimes risk means self-disclosure—but not the faux vulnerability that sheds tears and manipulates emotions but exposes us to no risk. That's simply a calculated self-disclosure under the guise of vulnerability. True confession involves risks. It's not designed as a transaction where we purchase reconciliation or the sympathy of followers. Vulnerability is an invitation to walk in integrity before God, regardless of the response from others.

Leading from inadequacy makes us vulnerable. *When inadequacy and vulnerability marry, weakness is conceived.*

THE WONDER OF WEAKNESS

The Corinthian troublers could brook no weakness. They were too accustomed to looking at a leader's appearance and gifts. They assumed that treasure was always stored within strength. They led from a different worldview and toward an opposing conspiracy. Let's call it the *Corinthian* conspiracy.

Here was their false formula: <u>My Strength</u> + God's Power = Resilience.

But this is just another earthly scheme that magnifies human might. Rather than acknowledging our clay pot, we polish it. And even try to pass it off as a gold-plated chalice.

Why is it so easy to believe the Corinthian conspiracy? I naturally fall into it. Not long ago I was having blood pressure issues. It would jack up and then drop down low. At first, I didn't know what was triggering it. I just knew that it was really hard to get off the couch. When lifting the TV remote becomes the hardest work you do, weakness becomes your cellmate. Then it's a good idea to ask for prayer. Or seek help. Unless you are proud. And foolish. Like me.

I found myself reluctant to share my condition with other people. I didn't want to talk about it, I didn't want to ask for prayer, I just wanted to tough it out. I work with a lot of young pastors—much younger. Who wants to be *that* old guy telegraphing his age?

Eventually, by God's grace, I saw my folly. It was nothing more than my pride, nothing more than my desire to appear strong, to look good, to keep my clay pot polished in the eyes of others. I wanted my ministry to be shining, to appear unbreakable. I didn't want other people to see my vulnerabilities—to see the cracks. *Yep, take a look, folks—a ministry crackpot, in the flesh!* No way.

So I instinctively tried to control perception by verbally polishing the pot. Can you relate? But as I get older, I see more. I notice that the leaders committed to polishing don't seem to finish well. When we want to be a big deal, it pretty much commits us to a life of polished performances. It makes us less relatable, less accessible, probably less accountable too. Because nobody really knows us, nobody around us is qualified to supply care and nobody around us is capable of understanding our unique cracks. Nobody is capable of really speaking wisdom to us. We embrace the Corinthian conspiracy: support my vision, ignore my cracks, and don't smear the polish.

If you're a leader and you feel uncomfortable reading these words, maybe it's because you're missing the wonder that leads you to the place of God's power. Don't despair. God's grace is greater than our sin or our foolishness. God's grace is more magnificent than our weakness. Whatever haunts you about your past performance or dogs you about your present impact, whenever you think your life is too messy or your leadership too lame, remember this one thing:

The perfection of Christ is greater than the cracks in your pot.

Jesus is not intimidated by your limitations or surprised by your struggles. The King has a deeper work, and his plans are unstoppable. Christ's grace is greater than your guilt; his steadfast love is greater than your shame. The finished work of Jesus frees him to rush to your side, to pour out his grace, to grant you the hope and perspective you need to see the wonder of his conspiracy—the remarkable plan illustrated by the shepherd who stumbled across the Dead Sea Scrolls: the surprising plot to store treasure in clay pots.

Christ loves us so much that we can stand secure in his embrace. God's power is greater than our weakness.

But if we truly want to connect our clay pot to power, we must renounce our polishing and move toward another plan. The second wonder is the one that reveals how God releases the treasure placed within the pot. This wonder helps us to comprehend how leaders bear pain as a means to flourish and how that part of the clay pot conspiracy makes us more like Jesus.

Are you ready? Then take a deep breath. A startling plunge awaits us.

QUESTIONS FOR REFLECTION

1. Make a list of some of the worldly credentials you most rely upon to feel good about your ministry.
2. How would your ministry change if you viewed weakness as your core credential?
3. In what ways might your present view of weakness stoke fatigue more than resilience?

Wonder #2
MAKE DEATH PRODUCE LIFE

The detective stood motionless in our living room. Uncomprehending, I asked him to say it again. He nodded and repeated, "Your daughter has passed away."

Reality boomeranged out, circled back, then clobbered me. Our haunting fear was realized. The addiction had won.

As I sit here today, trying to write out this story, the entire twisted journey feels utterly indescribable, or at least, beyond any categories of parenting, leadership, or life for which I was prepared. Programs, doctors, medication, counselors, interventions—we tried it all. Our daughter was deeply loved and hopelessly lost. We felt powerless as we watched the addiction grow voracious, consuming her drive, her dreams, and finally, her personality. Her suffering became our cross to bear. If you're a parent, you understand.

Addiction soaks clay pots in complexity. Brokenness pours out. Our journey brought us into parts of this sad world we never dreamed we would encounter. Dark places with desperate people became familiar terrain. Months bled into years as we fought for her life. Then death won. But not entirely—each morning I stare into the eyes of her son, now entrusted to us to raise.

Since that day, I've learned a lot about the weakness that comes with grief. Grief creeps up and seizes a moment, an hour, an afternoon. It attacks meaning and motivation. I think it's going to be like this for a while. The shadow of death, the empty chair, the burden of shame, the clay pot, broken.

Ministry, if I'm honest, is conflicting. It's been more splendid than I possibly expected, and more painful than I ever dreamed. Somewhere along the way, I began to think differently about resilience. It's no longer the place I am longing to reach after seasons of suffering or grief, a place where I "arrive" on the other side of trials. Learning about the conspiracy changed all of that. Resilience is the work of God, in and through mystery and agony—within both the world and church—by which he helps me persevere. It's God's work to make sure that I don't just squeak by but endure in a way that reveals his unexpected power.

This brings us to our next wonder. The wonder of death producing life. Prepare yourself. It's painfully exquisite.

THE WONDER: MAKE DEATH PRODUCE LIFE

Let's return to Paul's ministry. The influencers in Corinth were known for boasting about their power and for trash-talking incessantly about their leadership triumphs. So Paul says to them, in effect, "Let me share with you my ministry profile." He then supplies four surprising contrasts that form the basis of his boasting (2 Corinthians 4:8–9). Paul's vision of gospel leadership is nothing like that of his critics:

- *We are afflicted in every way, but not crushed.* Affliction refers to pressure, to feeling squeezed. Today, I boarded an aircraft to fly far away and do ministry for which I was unprepared. In a sense, I'm already airborne . . . *because I'm flying by the seat of my pants*! I feel the squeeze—ministry seems hard-pressed right now. I'm sure you've also had that anxious feeling when you realize the fire is growing and you're still looking for the extinguisher. There is pressure in ministry and in life where we feel gripped, squeezed. Paul says, "That's me. I'm squeezed—but not squashed."

- *Perplexed, but not in despair.* To be perplexed is to feel cornered or baffled. We can all relate to this. Leadership is often ambiguous and complex. Sometimes you feel like the only thing you can add is ignorance. *That's it, that's all I've got!* Bafflement hops in behind your mental steering wheel and starts driving you crazy. The autopilot is set toward misery. But Paul doesn't give in. He says, "Sure I'm perplexed. But I'm not driven to despair."
- *Persecuted, but not abandoned.* Paul is not referring to some kind of figurative persecution. Paul is not saying he "feels" wounded. He's not talking about what we may feel from criticism or people leaving over decisions we've made. Paul had actual enemies who not only slandered him, but physically attacked him. They beat him almost to death with rods and rocks. Yet he says, "I'm not abandoned. I'm never forsaken."

I marvel at Paul's resilience. Honestly, my "feeling-forsaken" switch gets flipped far too easily. Too often I go from seeing my flaws and faults to feeling forgotten. But Paul knew the gospel. He knew *Christ* was forsaken *for* him so that *he* would *never* be forsaken. Because Jesus cried out, "My God, my God, why have you forsaken me?" his leaders will never be alone. It's the wonder of God's inextinguishable, presence—bringing power for perseverance.

- *Struck down, but not destroyed.* The literal phrasing here is "but *by no means* destroyed." The word "struck" means to be whacked with a weapon. It may refer to Acts 14:19 where Paul was stoned and dragged outside the city of Lystra. He was left there for dead. But he lived. There was a form of resurrection—Paul got up. He took the blow, but was not destroyed. Paul kept on going.

For Paul, ministry was life spent in a clay jar. Each morning, he greeted a new day of leadership—and with it, his own inadequacy. Yet being afflicted, baffled, persecuted, and struck down was no mere occupational hazard. Paul discovered it was *essential* to a powerful, enduring ministry. Crazy as it may sound, Paul accepted that a *vital* part of his job description was: "We always carry around in our body the death of Jesus" (2 Corinthians 4:10 NIV).

Why is "carrying death in the body" so important? He answers in the verse that follows: "So that *his life* may *also* be revealed in our mortal body" (NIV, emphasis added).

Okay, let's tap the brakes. There's a lot of important clay pot stuff happening here. Paul seems to be saying that ministry is the exact opposite of the self-celebrating, platform-building, boasting that characterized the false teachers. Leadership, according to Paul, meant carrying death in his body. Yet God supplied enough power for Paul that, even though he was hard-pressed, perplexed, persecuted, and struck down, he was never crushed, despairing, forsaken, or destroyed. He was durable; truly and remarkably resilient.

To say it simply, Paul's vision of leadership was to *carry death in your body so that God can display the life of Jesus.*

Does it sound like Paul has slipped a mental disc? But Paul isn't crazy. It's God's conspiracy. And Paul believed it so deeply that it formed his vision of leadership and the basis of his boasting. Two chapters later, Paul commends his leadership in ministry:

> But as servants of God we commend ourselves in every way: by great endurance, in afflictions,

hardships, calamities, beatings, imprisonments, riots, labors, sleepless nights, hunger; by purity, knowledge, patience, kindness, the Holy Spirit, genuine love; by truthful speech, and the power of God; with the weapons of righteousness for the right hand and for the left; through honor and dishonor, through slander and praise. We are treated as impostors, and yet are true; as unknown, and yet well known; as dying, and behold, we live; as punished, and yet not killed; as sorrowful, yet always rejoicing; as poor, yet making many rich; as having nothing, yet possessing everything. (2 Corinthians 6:4–10)

But you and I are not Paul, right? Doesn't that let us off the hook? After all Paul was a capital "A" apostle and holds a distinct and unrepeatable role in redemptive history. That makes his suffering unique, doesn't it? It's true that Paul's suffering was uniquely difficult. But suffering for leaders and pastors is universally common. Paul was in a different league of suffering than most leaders. But we're all playing the same game. And registering for that game comes with a call to carry death in our body.

Why is that true?

BROKEN POTS EMBODY GOD'S TREASURE

Well, let me answer with another question. Do you remember your conversion? What if the humility and dependence you displayed at that time—when God raided your heart and bankrupted your vault of self-reliance—was not simply a condition of conversion but also ongoing transformation? What if coming to know yourself as a broken and weak sinner in continual need of grace is the key to becoming a fruitful leader who lasts?

God is so committed to his people being gospel-grounded and dependent upon him that he designed leadership not merely to *proclaim* the gospel, but to *embody* it? What if the heart of leadership is more about becoming living displays of broken vitality? And what if by reenacting the gospel—more than just rehearsing it as an idea, but actually experiencing a lesser version of Christ's death and resurrection—leaders also encounter the renewing power that ensures their potency and perseverance?

It's a lot to process, I know. But understanding this wonder unlocks the whole conspiracy. It may bring new meaning to what you are suffering right now. I wish I had known this as a new pastor. It would have explained a lot, like one of my first messages.

The first time I preached as a lead pastor, my hopes were through the roof. *With all humility* (I assured myself) *this could be truly epic. My performance will supply overwhelming confirmation that I am God's man to lead our church into the future. My words might even kickstart a little revival. Heck, why not a big one! After all, real leadership means expressing urgent faith for monumental impact, right?*

Five minutes into the message, I lost my voice. As bad as you might imagine this being, it was much worse. I rasped through fifteen to twenty minutes, then wrapped it up. Humiliation owned me. I might as well have just walked around the church with a "kick me!" sign strapped across my chest. I vowed to never let this happen again.

Next week, it happened again.

My foray into full-time preaching was, to say it kindly, unspectacular. At least a heart attack while preaching would have won a sympathy vote! But I didn't get sympathy. At best, I got pity, in the form of encouraging notes informing me that folks were praying for my nervousness, my anxiety, *my weak voice*. I wanted to come off looking like a pro. God decided to spotlight my rookie-ness. I longed to be seen as strong. But God was starting me on the journey toward weakness.

It's funny, but I thought leadership was going to polish my pot. God had other designs, including silencing one brand of confidence to cultivate another.

SUFFERING REFLECTS DEATH

Honestly, public discomfort or embarrassment are relatively mild on the weakness scale. Some experience weakness from opposition and persecution. That was the case for Paul, Peter, and many New Testament leaders. But mild or severe, one point remains incontrovertibly true: *Gospel ministry flows through clay pots who suffer.* "Share in suffering for the gospel by the power of God" (2 Timothy 1:8). Paul assumed that his call to ministry *meant* a call to suffer. "I was appointed a preacher and apostle and teacher," he says, "which is *why* I suffer as I do" (2 Timothy 1:11–12, emphasis added).

Suffering in ministry is not inherently glorious. We're not soldiers making sacrifices in battle for honor and glory. Like Paul, our present pain or shame is designed to produce leaders who embody the gospel message. It's the glory behind our second wonder. Our perfect and divine Savior was treated as a cursed criminal and subjected to slaughter, right before his startling, triumphant resurrection. His victory now animates our present and future with life. Christ's work is now wholly completed.

Yet here's the wonder beyond Christ's work: *The paradigm of dying and rising forms the pathway through ministry and the power for ministry.*

Many men sign up for pastoring pretty clueless about the core of their call. Paul Miller puts it this way: "To believe the gospel necessarily leads to entering into Christ's dying and rising. Knowing Jesus in these two complementary ways makes our knowledge of him richer, more complete. We embrace the whole pattern of Jesus's life story as the story of our own life."[1]

Ministry becomes a gospel reenactment in the life of the leader where God puts us through little "deaths" so that gospel life might flow. It's a series of trials where your kids see you maligned, but you do not retaliate; where one sleepless night rolls into the next; where you keep loving when you feel like your heart is empty. Yes, even in unexpected seasons where we grieve crippling losses, as we receive a "death sentence" and patiently wait to see what God will resurrect in its place, our Lord is at work. A stage for life is being set.

It all originates in the larger conspiracy. Death is at work "so that the life of Jesus also may be manifested in our mortal flesh" (2 Corinthians 4:11).

Do you see the plan? Leaders carry death to convey life. They suffer to thrive. *God breaks the pot to free the power.*

That's right. Your weaknesses and struggles—the very places your mind is going as you read this chapter—are the places God makes his power known most clearly. You are walking the path behind Paul. "I carry death, so that the life of Christ may be manifested in me."

It's strange, isn't it? We come into leadership thinking the kingdom advances through strong people using their amazing gifts to bear epic fruit. But God says, "Not really. When I want to shape a soul to lead, I bid him come and die. When I want my gospel to ring forth, *I shatter the jar.*"

Remember the shepherd boy in the last chapter? When he pitched that rock into the cave, he heard the pot fracture. Now we have the Dead Sea Scrolls—all because a pot was broken. Well, God lets his own stones fly. In their own way, they're far harder stones, with even deeper purposes. They're stones of hurt, discouragement, disappointment, and confusion. They're stones of illness, disability, and relational brokenness. Questions that are never answered. Closure that doesn't come. Relationships that dissipate, and dreams that are never realized. Stones break the pot and the shards of our inadequacy litter the ground—yet the cracks are all aglow with the promise of life.

BROKEN POTS ENCOUNTER RESURRECTION LIFE

Have you ever had a ministry experience that left you crushed with discouragement? Driven to despair? Or made you feel so stigmatized that it felt like a sentence of death hung over your life?

Paul could relate. Read these words slowly and take in the significance of what he is saying. Ponder each phrase, line by line.

> For we do not want you to be unaware, brothers, of the affliction we experienced in Asia. For we were so utterly burdened beyond our strength that we despaired of life itself. Indeed, we felt that we had received the sentence of death. (2 Corinthians 1:8–9a)

This account is astonishing. While commentators seem unclear on the nature of the affliction, we are not left to speculate over the emotional impact.

- "utterly burdened beyond our strength"
- "we despaired of life itself"
- "we felt that we had received the sentence of death"

Paul is not reciting a list of the customary trials that shadow every pastor. This is devastation. This is a description of the unguarded moments when ministry crashes through the door and delivers a kind of death. Lead for more than a few years and you know exactly what that means. Some of us are there right now.

But wait. The story turns in an unexpected direction. The clay pot conspiracy is revealed. Life follows death: "But that was to make us rely not on ourselves but on God who raises the dead. He delivered us from such a deadly peril, and he will deliver us. On him we have set our hope that he will deliver us again" (2 Corinthians 1:9b–10).

There was a deeper design behind Paul feeling like he was sentenced to death. God was at work reminding Paul that being emotionally crushed is not the end, but a new beginning. There was a plan for Paul's despair and devastation, a wonder to be revealed: God would make death produce life. "That was to make us rely not on ourselves but on God who raises the dead."

This lands as audacious. *Wait just a minute! Are you suggesting God intentionally brought Paul to a place of weakness; a place of despair; a place that felt like emotional death?*

To which I would say: yes, exactly!

God broke the pot to make a point. He was setting the stage for a resurrection. "He delivered us from such a deadly peril, *and he will deliver us.* On him we have set our hope that he will deliver us again." Paul's darkest moments became a tutorial on trust followed by a glorious deliverance. "There is always design in our distress," Sam Storms observed. "God so values our trust in him alone that he will graciously dismantle everything else in the world that we might be tempted to rely on: even life itself, if necessary. His desire is that we grow deeper and stronger in our confidence that he himself is all we need."[2]

Do you see the conspiracy at work? God designs ministry to deepen our confidence in him. He will work to make the man like the gospel. We suffer; we die; we are resurrected. We learn to anticipate resurrection, hope for deliverance, and embody the transformational gospel we are called to proclaim. Experiences that feel like death nurture gospel confidence. Then we become gospel templates in the service of others. "So death is at work in us, but life in you" (2 Corinthians 4:12).

Who knew? The cracks within the clay are now unmistakable. But through the work of the artist, the light of the gospel shines through. Jesus becomes brighter as he shines his light through his weak servants. Weak leaders make for stronger, more resilient ministries. These ministries learn to rely on the power of Christ, not human strength. Our souls are fortified through accepting the call to death and resurrection. God makes death produce life.

Sure, it's confounding. But that's because it's God's conspiracy.

> Our Weakness + God's Power = Resilient Ministry

BEING BROKEN MAKES US STRONGER

There's one final thing we don't want to miss: Human weakness is *not* the wonder. The wonder comes in the way these gospel reenactments make us stronger and more resilient. *It's the amazing way that God binds the broken to make us more durable.*

Have you ever seen a pot repaired through *kintsugi*? *Kintsugi* is the Japanese art of mending pottery by carefully reattaching the broken pieces with a bright gold lacquer. Through the repair, the brokenness is not hidden, but highlighted and fortified. Tracing the damage displays a resurrection. The pot has been reconstituted and made more durable and resilient. The artist uses the restoration to tell a story of redemption. A pot was broken. Now it lives on, stronger than ever.

Pastor, here is the marvel: Your suffering is not an obstacle to resilience; it's designed to produce the strength to help you finish well.

> Count it all joy, my brothers, when you meet trials of various kinds, for you know that the testing of your faith produces steadfastness. And let steadfastness have its full effect, that you may be perfect and complete, lacking in nothing. (James 1:2–4)

This point has never been more important for pastors than at this very moment. Ministry today is becoming more psychologized, captivating pastors with therapeutic categories and convincing us we are being ruined by suffering. We fear that insults, failures, and betrayals inflict lasting injury.

The message being reinforced is, *what doesn't kill us, enfeebles us.* Pain and problems make colossal withdrawals from the bank account of resilience. Your balance is getting perilously low. Narratives constantly reaffirm the voice in our heads: *I should be protected from people's sin. I should not be subject to others' emotional reactions and ugly behavior. Ministry should be a safe space.* This is the story we too easily begin to tell ourselves.

I'm not suggesting we blow up the idea of safe spaces. I want my grandson in a safe space when I check him into school or a kid's ministry. I want to know that counselors can keep a confidence and aren't blogging the names of folks who seek their help. But being safe from pain, hurt, toxicity, even physical threats was never part of the ministry contract. "For to this you have been called, because Christ also suffered for you, leaving you an example, so that you might follow in his steps" (1 Peter 2:21).

We're not unique, you know. What do cops, firemen, and paramedics have in common with ministers? We each signed up to run toward suffering, not away from it. There are certain vocations where safety must be sacrificed in the service of others. Sure, pastors aren't dodging bullets in the same way other vocations do. At least not in the West. But when Paul calls Timothy to sacrificial ministry, the metaphor he borrows punctuates this very point. "Share in suffering as a good soldier of Christ Jesus" (2 Timothy 2:3).

There are mental and physical costs to wading into people's worst moments. There are costs to disappointing their expectations, standing in opposition to community injustice, admonishing a church member for their sin, and telling a husband it's time to treat his wife better. People may use you, betray you, slander you, and play by a different set of rules. There are also spiritual attacks, bouts of anxiety, criticism from others, and mental anguish that accompany the call to preach and pastor. Pastoral training should jettison the illusion of safety and import suffering-preparation into their program.

Don't get me wrong. As a pastor, you will be satisfied and experience joy in ways you never dreamed possible. Through these trials, life will be revealed in your mortal body. Gospel blood will course through your veins and invigorate your ministry. You will not merely endure. Your ministry will grow stronger through the Spirit's *kintsugi*.

But you will not be safe.

Do you see where this is going? If dependence upon God is the point, weakness becomes an asset. Weakness is the space where reliance is built and grace is delivered. Your burdens and pain are not obstacles to resilience. They're *the means of producing it*. God reconstitutes the leader's weakness for our good and his glory. It's all part of God's conspiracy, where "suffering produces endurance, and endurance produces character, and character produces hope" (Romans 5:3–4).

God breaks the pot to shape the soul. It's a mysterious grace we are given, a grace upon which we stand.

THE PERFECT POT BROKEN

If your ministry feels broken and you're wondering how this could possibly be part of God's plan to strengthen you, remember: Your pot is not the first to be broken. The clay pot of Christ's body was crushed for our sins. Then he rose from death on the third day. It's the conspiracy's origin—at the cross, God made death produce life. It was the plan Satan never saw coming. And it changes everything.

Paul describes this later in 2 Corinthians, "He was crucified in weakness, yet he lives by God's power" (13:4). Christ's weakness described here is not from fallenness or moral frailty. No, Christ emptied himself and assumed the poverty of humanity. His origin story dripped with scandal. Jesus was born in the obscurity of Bethlehem and then raised across the tracks in Nazareth. Our Savior would hardly strike cultural influencers as a specimen of human strength. Centuries before he was born, Isaiah predicted his weakness and frailty:

> He had no form or majesty that we should look at him,
> and no beauty that we should desire him.
> He was despised and rejected by men,
> a man of sorrows and acquainted with grief;

and as one from whom men hide their faces
   he was despised, and we esteemed him not.
                                   (Isaiah 53:2b–3)

Weakness continues through the manner of this death. A man suspended from a cross, by the standards of Roman law and Jewish custom, was a criminal. Crucifixion was a disgraceful form of punishment, a symbol of the curse writ large over his entire existence.

No one observing the spectacle of this crucifixion would see a champion, a victor, a messiah. None would glory in the one who suffers there. The cross screams defeat and brokenness. Only weakness is on parade. Carl Trueman observes,

> Suffering and weakness are not just that way in which Christ triumphs and conquers; they are the way in which we are to triumph and conquer too. In other words, if suffering and weakness are the ways God works in Christ, it is to be expected that these are the ways he will work in those who seek to follow Christ.
>
> One does not become a theologian by knowing a lot about God; one becomes a theologian by suffering the torments and feeling the weakness

which union with Christ must inevitably bring in its wake.³

Jesus took the worst we could do to him and miraculously turned it into the very best he could do for us. The power of the gospel comes from the weakness of the cross. It is through the foolishness of the cross that God's strength meets our frailty, and we find hope. It's through brokenness—just like the shepherd boy broke that pot many years ago to reveal the scrolls—that others see the treasure.

It's a conspiracy of hope for those struggling in ministry, and it's a conspiracy of hope for those who have failed: My weakness *plus* God's power *equals* endurance in hope!

REDEEMING BROKENNESS

Leaders, don't begrudge the nails that pin you to the cross. Don't despise the "death sentences" hanging over you. From the ashes of your brokenness, God is kindling the fires of hope and deliverance. Though it baffles the mind, these wounds are building the resilience you seek. These wounds are preparing your soul to meet your Savior. Each day in heaven will be more glorious because of what you have borne on earth.

I can't even begin to understand the purposes of God in my daughter's tragic death. But that doesn't paralyze me. Though God's intent is inscrutable, the effects are undeniable. First, the window into my own inadequacy has expanded. After all, loving an addict is inadequacy personified. It's like watching someone you love being slowly devoured behind a locked door.

But even inadequacy has a use. My inadequacy pressed me into the arms of Christ. I relied on him in ways I never had in the past. Sadly, the story didn't end with her glorious deliverance. This remains my burden to bear. Some days it is heavier than others. But the wonder helps me to trust that God is at work bringing life from death, even when I don't see it.

Deliverance will come in ways I never imagined and in places I never conceived. When I cherish her memory, my eyes turn inward, upward, and forward once again. God brought me through catastrophe into new life. My experience is a metaphor that points to the true death and resurrection. Because he died and lived, so can I. And if his resurrection power has shone through my clay pot, who can say what life he will bring through a family tragedy?

When I look into my grandson's eyes and see my daughter, the pang reminds me that God breaks the pot to free his power. If you're in ministry and experiencing any kind of loss or weakness, there is more to talk about and more you need to hear. But for now, hear this: *The breaking in your life is forging a more durable soul*, the kind of soul that reminds the world of the true power behind a crucified Savior.

My weakness *plus* God's power *equals* my resilience. It's the clay pot conspiracy. And it is magnificent!

QUESTIONS FOR REFLECTION

1. What are some of the expectations you brought with you into ministry and leadership?
2. Reflect on a time where you felt like you were "carrying in the body the death of Jesus" (2 Corinthians 4:10). What were the circumstances? How did you feel?
3. When you think of that season, how did God deliver you? If you are still struggling in the midst of this circumstance, in what ways do you see God creating reliance and deepening your dependence upon him?

Wonder #3
LET REPENTANCE STOKE RESILIENCE

It's been a peculiar afternoon. After a wonderful church service, I drove the goodwill straight off a cliff by expressing some justifiable annoyance at Kimm. "Justifiable annoyance" is what happens when a husband uncorks a jug of arrogance and pours it on his wife. Annoyances are justifiable, more or less, in proportion to the man's stupidity.

Today I felt very "justified." A true knucklehead.

Kimm knew the drill. She eventually rewound the tape, reminded me of the things I said, and paired it with other recent incidents. As I listened, the moral high ground disintegrated beneath my feet. An hour ago, I was convinced I was right. Now after listening and repenting, my error stuns me.

You'd think someone married over forty years and in ministry almost as long would be wiser. You might also think that writing marriage books and conducting marriage events for so long would mean I've cracked the code. But honestly, I see way more sin in my life now than when we were first married. Maturity hasn't resulted in a shorter list of sins. God's work over the years has sharpened my eyesight and converted a general sense of my sin into something with scope and surgical specificity.

How does a pastor respond to an ever-deepening awareness of their own sin? Do we become overscrupulous, assuaging our guilt by identifying ourselves as failures? Do we shrink back and submit to Satan's accusation that we are hypocrites? Or is it possible that repentance catapults us, not into hypocrisy nor failure, but down a surprising pathway toward resilience?

In this chapter we will explore how sin surfaces in the clay pot. We will uncover how sin operates in your self-diagnostics—where you see it and how you interpret it. And there is one titanic reason why exploring sin makes our list of seven wonders.

The biggest threat to endurance is not your limitations. It's not your constitution, your family of origin, your physical maladies, or your Enneagram number. No: *The biggest threat to leadership resilience is our unrelenting battle against indwelling sin.*

SIN ATTACKS ENDURANCE THROUGH DECEPTION

Sin deceives us. Creation contains the record of sin's origins with these words, "Now the serpent was more crafty" (Genesis 3:1). Satan twists God's Word and reinterprets God's heart: *You should have more. Paradise is not enough. God fears your potential.* Sin cons, then consumes. It deceives, then devours. "Oh, take heed of Satan's first motions to sin," observed Thomas Watson. "He is first a *fox*, and then a *lion*."[1] The fox and lion sought to devour me today. No clay pot lies beyond its reach.

And, just to make things even harder, original sin has installed a cloaking device in every human heart. Sin committed becomes sin concealed. Rendering sinners "clueless" is part of the very character and core of the fall.

Blame-shifting—"The woman whom you gave to be with me, she gave me fruit of the tree, and I ate" (Genesis 3:12)—is the reaction of the first human being caught in sin. What we witness here is not the *event* of sin, mind you. Adam and Eve have already swallowed the hook baited by Satan. No, here we trace the swelling *effects* of the event, how culpable creatures respond when creation is corrupted. Truth is suppressed to conceal sin and divert blame. Just listen to Adam—his blame-game crackles with deception.

The first deceit filled clay pots with iniquity. The second put a lid over the contents. And no one is immune.

Years later, King David becomes outraged when Nathan tells him about a self-indulgent rich man who steals a poor man's beloved lamb to feed his wealthy guests. He cannot brook this tragic injustice. "As the LORD lives," cries David, "the man who has done this deserves to die" (2 Samuel 12:5). But the plot has a twist—David is the man! Covetousness, sexual assault, murder, and hypocrisy has fogged over his moral windshield. Nathan creates an allegory to pierce the darkness of David's deception.

Sound familiar? It's Eden: The Sequel. Once unleashed into a fallen world, sin deceives us by erasing our agency and convincing us that we are entitled to the things we want. Once deluded, entitlement empowers our injustice until we devour others: Adam toward Eve; David toward Bathsheba and Uriah, me toward Kimm.

Deception undermines relationships and handicaps our resilience. Moral ambiguity paralyzes progress. Leadership becomes tedious. "Thorns and snares are in the way of the crooked" (Proverbs 22:5). As we sow to our sinful nature, we reap bondage. Sin attacks our endurance as the effort to prop up our delusions and manage the collateral damage from our entitlement becomes utterly exhausting.

SIN ATTACKS ENDURANCE THROUGH EXHAUSTION

Denying sin is exhausting. When the clay pot fills with lies, stress widens the cracks.

David eventually understood. "For when I kept silent, my bones wasted away through my groaning all day long. For day and night your hand was heavy upon me; my strength was dried up as by the heat of summer" (Psalm 32:3–4).

Wasted bones. Groaning lips. Dried-up strength. David is describing the effect of guilt and shame as physical and spiritual *exhaustion*. In this fallen world, our physical condition remains inextricably bound to our moral decisions. Both weights and sins impact our progress (Hebrews 12:1). Brokenness burdens us. I get it. The hours between sinning against Kimm and confessing to her were emotionally and physically exhausting. Sure, my soul sinned. But my body kept the score.

There's an age thing too. Earlier I mentioned maturity has not condensed my sin list. God converted me, but he intentionally left the battle with sin as part of my story. That's why, as a seasoned leader, Paul referred to himself as "the foremost" of sinners (1 Timothy 1:15–16). I think God wrote our imperfections into our story because weaknesses glorify him more than sinlessness. Our brokenness moves us toward humility and dependence, not moral perfection. "If the story of redemption is about Jesus and his righteousness," said Barbara Duguid, "then our continuing weakness actually shines the spotlight on Jesus all the more brightly."[2] Jesus said it this way to Paul, "My power is made perfect in weakness" (2 Corinthians 12:9).

Pray for the leader who thinks he must model sinless strength rather than dependent weakness. The scorch of that spotlight dries the soul. Uzziah found out. "But when he was strong, he grew proud, to his destruction. For he was unfaithful to the LORD his God and entered the temple of the LORD to burn incense on the altar of incense" (2 Chronicles 26:16). Being strong made Uzziah proud. Pride lowered the gate for compromise to raid his heart. Destruction followed. The wise leader understands the devastation concealed within strength.

Maybe you can relate to this right now. Your following is large but your faithfulness is weak. You are strong, but quite honestly, not resilient. You know it because while you are reading this book, the Holy Spirit

LET REPENTANCE STOKE RESILIENCE

is reading you. People know you only as a saint, never a sinner. You're Uzziah and you're exhausted. Stay tuned—there's really good news.

Maybe there is a breeze of conviction blowing through your mind as you read—whispers of a deceptive pattern, an inordinate desire, a lingering disobedience. Please don't stop reading. God's love for you is greater than you can possibly fathom. The shame you feel is the Accuser, not the Savior. Yep, more weight. The conscience, too, is capricious. It can alert us to sins, but it won't escort us to Christ. When we try to ignore it, along come self-hatred, crushing shame, unrelenting condemnation. These deep feelings can be creative acts of self-atonement—the soul's attempt to pay the price for sins apart from the Savior. But paying an impossible debt is an unreachable goal, wholly and fully exhausting.

God will persist in pursuing you—he will dispense grace, not to bully, but to guide. "When my spirit faints within me, you know my way!" (Psalm 142:3). You want God's way. Bible passages will glow brighter because of the Spirit's conviction. Hope will kindle within your heart. Does that describe you right now? You can be freed from the weight of fatigue or humiliation that you now feel. I want to share some simple steps you can take. But first, let's look at one more erosion of endurance.

OUR RESPONSE TO BEING SINNED AGAINST DEPLETES US

The greatest hazard to our future flourishing is how we deal with the past and present effects of sin. Not just ours. This includes the sins of others too. Because to lead is to be sinned against.

Maybe you are stuck in bitterness over the way you have been treated. Terrible things happened. You or someone you love were harmed. Debased. Victimized. Your memory holds you captive and anger, guilt, and shame are welded to your prison bars. The biggest hurdle for your resilience is the wrong done against you by someone else.

Our stories of pain, brokenness, and weakness are significant. But our human weakness, or the way we have been sinned against by others, cannot destroy the soul. Only our sin does that.[3]

If you are a leader who has been sinned against in grievous ways, I hope you have someone you can sit with to share your heart and grieve your pain. Having people in my life with whom I can open my heart and acknowledge the reality of pain has comforted me on countless occasions. Much of this book, in fact, explores how God uses suffering in a leader's life to grow and enlarge his soul.

But for now, let me mention an important lesson I've learned over my many years of sinning, and being the object of other people's sin.

The enemy loves when we fixate upon the ways in which we have been sinned against. Being sinned against, or even just *feeling* like we have been sinned against, can make us think we have the permission to nurture a variety of soul-depleting responses. We enter our mental courtroom and repeatedly prosecute the accused in our own minds. But we feel worse, not better. We experience anger, not peace. Rather than satisfying justice, the scab has been ripped from the wound of injustice.

In the parable of the unforgiving servant, when the servant who was forgiven a great amount screams "Pay what you owe" into the face of one who owed him little, the result is bondage (Matthew 18:21–35). Jesus is not saying you can't be sinned against in life-impacting ways. Who knows more about being sinned against than Christ? No, Jesus is showing us the path toward flourishing in the face of being sinned against. He moves the gospel to the middle of our pain.

According to Christ, forgiveness and forward progress come only as we remember that our sins against God are our greatest debt. The gospel reminds us each day that God has forgiven us far more than we will ever know or could ever pay. Now he calls us to forgive, just as we have been forgiven.

By imprisoning the unforgiving man at the end of the story, Jesus reminds us that there is no such thing as justifiable bitterness. Resentment always shackles us. We commit this moral crime expecting to imprison another. But our soul shrivels while we wait for their incarceration. One of the worst lies in the history of the world is that we can use our bitterness to punish the one who hurt us.

And yet, even deeper, the largest threat to our resilience lies not in what's been done *to us* by others, but in forgetting what's been done *for us* by Christ. When we withhold forgiveness from others, we enslave ourselves again to sin. Worse than that—we take hands which were freed from chains and use them as manacles to choke fellow servants.

The cross, however, strips all sin of power—both our sins and that of others. They lose the muscle to take us down. Jesus embodied perfect innocence as he perfectly obeyed God's law in all things at all times. Yet the greatest injustice in the history of the world was committed when the sinless Lamb was "pierced for *our* transgressions, [and] crushed for *our* iniquities" (Isaiah 53:5, emphasis added). Christ suffered injustice to save *us* from *justice*. And that wondrous juxtaposition unleashed kingdom power upon all who treasure Christ—both sinners and sinned against.

But that's not all. Christ's past now courses through our story, forging our pain into a new identity. We are no longer bound to the evil in others. Christ allows us to acknowledge the depravity of life without removing God from the picture. We can say with Joseph, "You meant evil against me, but God meant it for good" (Genesis 50:20).

This week I sat with a leader who had endured slander, betrayal, and ugly hostility from other believers in his small town. Now, a year later, he was sitting across from me celebrating how God had given him peace and faith. At first, the injustices surrounded and hounded him—they grew big, and God became small. But the gospel slowly reshaped his paradigm.

Through Christ, God had forgiven him an incalculable debt; he was now gospel-bound to do the same. Cataloging how he was sinned against depleted and defeated him. The gospel supplied the power to tear away the tentacles of bitterness. His circumstances did not change, at least not immediately. But God empowered him to change his response. Turning his soul away from what he could not control (the events of evil) and toward what he could control (responding with the gospel and trusting God meant it for good) provided a pathway out of the pit. Elizabeth Elliot explains this by saying, "I find that events do not change souls. It is our response to them which finally affects us."[4]

THE WONDER: LET REPENTANCE STOKE ENDURANCE

How does seeing more sin or being repeatedly sinned against not hollow out our resilience? There is one response to our sinful desires and our sinful responses to the hard things that happen to us which opens up a refreshing stream of life and vitality.

The response is *repentance*.

Repentance means confessing our specific sin to God, believing the guarantee of Christ's forgiveness, and applying God's Word to change our thinking and practice.

Sin always subverts God's good things with the promise that vice will deliver a greater delight. Adam and Eve swapped enjoying God in the garden for fruit-tasting. The wonder of repentance includes how it catalyzes the conviction of sin so the confession of wrong becomes the experience of grace. For me, true repentance means future disagreements with Kimm will be marked by more gentleness and less harshness, more humility and less arrogance.

LET REPENTANCE STOKE RESILIENCE

When was the last time you heard the word *repentance* in a conversation or a sermon? When was the last time you used it in reference to yourself? "The problem is," observed J. I. Packer, "that teaching, talk and thought about repentance have virtually vanished, not just from our post-Christian secular world, but from the lives of church people too."[5] Why is this so? And how does repentance help a leader's soul to rebound?

Our clay pots are brimming with sins. Ironically, the more we see of Christ, the more we see of our sins. As we behold the glory of God in the face of Jesus Christ, dark places within the heart are seen more clearly. When I became a Christian, I did ask for forgiveness for my sins, but I did not begin to perceive the deep veins of sin that coursed through my heart. It has taken a lifetime to understand Jeremiah's observation that "The heart is deceitful above all things, and desperately sick; who can understand it?" (Jeremiah 17:9). As I shared, I am still seeing new areas where I go my own way and not God's way. I'm still a sheep that likes to wander. New seasons of life bring new temptations.

So what keeps our expanding understanding of sin from becoming crushing condemnation? What uncages the gospel when sin's magnitude threatens our soul?

It's the wonder of repentance. When sin boils within me, repentance kills the heat. But it's more than lowering the heart's thermostat. Repentance also refreshes the soul with streams of forgiveness and grace. David experienced it. "I acknowledged my sin to you, and I did not cover my iniquity; I said, 'I will confess my transgressions to the LORD,' and you forgave the iniquity of my sin" (Psalm 32:5).

Repentance unlocks grace. And grace is the fuel for the engine of resilience. The first of Luther's ninety-five theses, nailed to the Wittenberg church door in 1517, declared: "When our Lord and Master Jesus Christ said, 'Repent' [Matthew 4:17], he willed that the whole life of believers should be one of repentance." Luther wanted a reformation where grace was cemented into the believer's foundation. To achieve it, the church needed a broader understanding of sin and a constant experience of the wonder of repentance.

A lifestyle of repentance makes the gospel even more precious to ponder, more startling to behold. The expanding record of our debts—our failure to obey God's law—is already stamped "paid in full" by the blood of Christ. Our sins can be unmasked as ugly and horribly dishonorable because God's punishment for our moral failures has been fully satisfied; our burden of shame has already been swapped out for Christ's perfect righteousness. Resilience flows to the soul as we draw near to his throne of grace, receiving mercy and grace to help in our time of need (Hebrews 4:16).

WALK TOWARD THE WONDER

Maybe you are reading this and feeling under the conviction of sin. Maybe you have a hidden sin that few know about, perhaps even a ministry-disrupting sin. Or maybe you are like me, prone to garden variety sins, like becoming quickly irritated, defensive, self-centered. Regardless of who you are or what sins are weighing you down, let's crank up the gospel-volume. That's right, flip the good news dial to maximum, and let the tune of God's grace overwhelm the sound of the evil one and his accusations. If you can't find the setting, let me help:

- Jesus loves you, and because he rose from the dead, he's praying for you (Hebrews 7:25).
- The random thoughts accusing you must be replaced by superior thoughts of God. Take them captive (2 Corinthians 10:5). Set your mind on better things (Colossians 3:2; Philippians 4:8).
- The judgments of others are a trial only for this life. God knows all (Psalm 139:1–4) and evaluates

you lovingly, graciously, and in light of his success upon the cross (Colossians 1:11–12).
- Failure attacks identity and seeks to rename you. But your mistakes cannot name you. God has already claimed you, and he calls you his child (Galatians 4:7).
- Your sins are not the final thing God speaks over your life or your future. As long as you draw breath, there is always more to God's story. There is always a next chapter (John 21:15–19).
- Don't sanitize your anger and resentment, and don't try to do this on your own. Find someone you trust and respect. Then "Confess your sins to one another and pray for one another, that you may be healed" (James 5:16). Confession of sin is a gracious wonder that unleashes healing.
- People talk and gossip hurts (Proverbs 10:18), but the cross reminds us that only a small portion of our mistakes and sins are ever really seen by others. Our sin was so bad it required God's blood to solve the problem (Hebrews 9:11–14).
- Don't lose heart. God often designs failure to produce what's necessary for us to finish the race. *Happy is the Christian who learns that God may incite desires he does not fully satisfy on earth.*

Maybe you need to think about that more today (2 Corinthians 4:16–18).
- Self-pity digs a hole in our story and seeks to bury us. The gospel speaks to self-pity by reminding us that even when life delivers a demoralizing blow, we have been treated far better than our sins deserve (Psalm 103:10).
- The gospel never says, "What if?" but always, "What now?" "What if?" shrinks the soul under the withering heat of vain speculation. "What now?" grounds us in the reality of a providential God superintending all things for our good (Romans 8:28) and asks "What should I now do to please God?" (Colossians 1:10; Hebrews 13:16).
- This is not your real home (2 Peter 3:13). Once you arrive safely home in the new heavens and new earth, you will see your failure through the eyes of eternity and stand amazed at how God used it for his glory (Isaiah 65:17; Revelation 2:1–7).

The gospel is the ultimate wisdom of God for our sins, no matter what they may be. It is God's reminder that our failures are never big enough to stall his love or stop his plans. Christ's power to keep us is greater than our pull toward sin. His finished work at the cross means we finish too.

I need to be reminded of that next time I uncork my ugly upon my bride. Maybe you need it right now too. Remember that *Christ* did not fail. He succeeded so our life and leadership can change. Starting now.

Because of the gospel, there is always hope, always rescue, always another chance. Draw near to him, and he will draw near to you. Let repentance stoke your resilience.

QUESTIONS FOR REFLECTION

1. How has your awareness of your own sin grown over the course of your ministry?
2. Think of a time in your leadership journey when you were sinned against. What was your response? What would you do differently?
3. What are some specific ways that repentance can be the most life-giving response to your own sin *and* to your experiences of being sinned against?

Wonder #4
LEARN LOVE WHEN THE CHURCH WOUNDS YOU

The last twelve years have formed a kind of trilogy—three personal stories where monumental loss met indomitable grace. Along the way, my wife Kimm and I crossed thresholds where one story ended, another began. My youngest daughter becoming pregnant with our grandson began a new book. Another opened around her tragic death when, in the blink of an eye, we became permanent caregivers for our grandson. A year later, we filed for adoption.

As I write those last few sentences, I'm struck by how difficult it is to share where this trilogy started. It's not an easy story to tell. I know I am an imperfect witness, indelibly influenced by my own perspective as I seek to explore the lineaments of a complicated history. There is no moral high ground, only broken people doing the best we could. But I see more clearly now that it has cost me to love the church, just as it has cost the church to love me. May God help me to magnify his grace as we explore this unexpected wonder.

THE NEXT UNEXPECTED WONDER

This story started many years ago at the first church I pastored. For a long period of time, local church life seemed to chug forward like we were ticketed passengers on the Blessing Express. Our family was comfortable, connected, and moving ahead. The train was familiar: other passengers were dear friends and frequent travelers with us, and the direction was one we anticipated. Part of the sheer joy in the trip was that we were all on the same train, traveling together, and moving in the same direction. I know there were ways I took pride in that.

Then the train crashed. Or rather, we jumped the tracks onto another train, with new passengers, heading in another direction. Thinking about this now simultaneously exhilarates and exhausts me. Over a decade later, I still feel like an exile in a strange land. But I get that. New journeys are often overrated. "We are plain quiet folk," explains Bilbo, "and have no use for adventures. Nasty disturbing uncomfortable things!"[1] But

God has his own agenda. Sometimes he invites us to leave home by making it impossible to stay.

That's what happened. Yet in our sojourn, we caught sight of a wonder—a North Star that guided us to the center of the conspiracy: *To truly love the church, we must come to terms with her imperfections.*

THE COST OF CARE

Any discussion of church imperfections must start with a mirror. We must stare unblinkingly at ourselves and say what we see. We lead as flawed men. Our identities become easily wrapped around the church axle. Our ungodly desires get in the way. Recently I had to confess to another leader that I had sinfully judged him. I wish I could say it was an isolated incident, but I have done it before. Like most church leaders, I long to lead wisely, but I find desires that keep me from doing the things I want to do (Galatians 5:17).

Pastors are not omniscient or omnicompetent, far from it. We are limited and fallible—flawed shepherds leading imperfect sheep.

We also feel deeply the call to love an imperfect church in the way Christ did. "Christ loved the church and gave himself up for her" (Ephesians 5:25). We recognize that the church Christ loved and died for did not start as the upgraded Bride "who has made herself ready" for Christ's return (Revelation 19:7). God saw us at our worst—the imperfect, malware-ridden 1.0 version, and chose us anyway. "But God shows his love for us in that while we were still sinners, Christ died for us" (Romans 5:8).

Pastoring is where an imperfect person leads imperfect people in an imperfect church to reach an imperfect world. We get it. Or at least we think we do.

Most pastors know this and would affirm it. We know we are called to join the fellowship of suffering, take up our cross, and follow Christ (Matthew 16:24). But what we don't expect is for the church to be a common source of our suffering. What we don't expect is how deep the church can cut. "When an enemy hurts you, that is bad," says Gavin Ortlund. "But when the *church* hurts you, the pain and disorientation are next-level."[2] Yet what's often missing is the wonder of what happens when church imperfections crash land into our lives. And the stupefying marvel of the deep work of God that occurs when her brokenness almost breaks you.

Imperfect means that, in a broken world, even the redeemed are unable to act completely consistently with all we say we believe. To illustrate that point, God uses sheep.

SHEEP WANDER

Sheep are prone to wander. Spring them from one hole and they will happily plunge into another. Sheep are led astray easily. There's a story about a ram named Errol who thought he could fly. He climbed a tree, jumped off a branch, and flapped his legs all the way down until he hit the ground. Apparently exhilarated by the experience, Errol taught more sheep how to fly. Carnage ensued. Upon seeing this, the shepherd decided to live a sheepless life.[3] The point? Be it flying or false teachers, sheep can be quickly baited to act against their own best interest.

TROUBLE APPEARS AND GRACE COMES ALONG TOO

Sheep and shepherds were not created for flight. To thrive, we must be grounded. That was my experience as a pastor for almost three decades. I was part of a thriving denomination started by godly men and women. The early days were marked by the beauty of rich doctrine, passionate worship, and deep relational attachments. Some of my most cherished memories in ministry—really, in life—are connected to the local church where I pastored and among the people we loved within our denomination.[4]

But eventually trouble appeared. One of the leaders of the network came under sharp criticism, sparked, in part, by an estranged leader who posted charges online. To ensure the charges could be investigated without the appearance of manipulating the outcome, the leader stepped aside. Suddenly, while I was on a vacation, I became the interim president and board chairman of this ministry. Never have I been more grateful for the word *interim*.

Confusion and chaos arrived soon after I stepped into my new role. Weaknesses long unaddressed within the ministry broke surface in a tsunami of criticism. Trust and confidence wavered. The founding church for the whole movement signaled an intent to leave and eventually did. National news outlets began to call. We had no policies to guide us through conflict or charges. Our leadership was imperfect. Things were messy.

Have you ever been in a complex leadership situation where you realize that regardless of what you do, people will be angry, hurt, or disappointed? Or maybe all three? That's where I landed. I never noticed how much I craved approval until it evaporated. For most of us, an absence of affirmation often reveals the presence of people-pleasing. In me it was deep and ugly. I felt like I was supposed to be the hero. I *wanted* to be the hero.

Thank God for our real Hero, who give us more grace in undeserving moments.

Grace, like manna, arrives for the moment and lasts for the day. We need new mercies each morning. Be it a prodigal child or organizational dysfunction, grace refuses easy answers and emboldens us to reckon with truth. As grace settles, we gain faith to acknowledge imperfections and limitations; to embrace complexity. Grace distributes enough clarity for next steps, but never enough to displace our reliance upon Jesus. By grace, we moved forward. Imperfectly.

We organized the board, sought counsel, and hired outside help from ministry specialists. They analyzed our systemic weaknesses and helped us find the right method for evaluating the charges against the leader. The conclusions of the independent review were published online, warts and all, and our founder was then methodically examined in light of the charges. The investigative panels cleared him, and he was returned to ministry.

It wasn't pretty. We had to face our organizational flaws. Still, encouraging things were happening and it seemed like the end of a hard, ugly season. But tucked within that chaos was a larger mess.

THE GRACE OF GOING FROM BAD TO WORSE

As you are reading my story, maybe you're wondering, "Is this guy just another cynical pastor going dark on the church?" We all know the profile. They love Jesus. But they're done with his bride.

It's true that I carry baggage. More than I even know. But I'm still a diehard local church dude. Test my DNA, and you will still find local church genes. I've been a member of a local church for over forty years and enjoyed pastoring for thirty-three years. Now I lead a global church planting network. And I'm helping to plant a church right now in my community. For almost four decades of local church leadership, I have been captivated by her beauty while also, like many, bloodied by her jagged edges.

Do you remember a time where you felt like you arrived at the bottom of a painful season, only to discover there were four more floors hidden beneath the cellar? That's what happened to us. Within the bedlam was an even deeper mess—a family crisis. Our daughter informed us that her marriage was capsizing. The details of her subsequent divorce belong to her and her ex-husband—it is their story to tell. But their separation had a polarizing impact upon a small but vocal group within our local church.

A perfect storm gathered. While leading our denomination through a calamitous national drama, our parenting came under intense scrutiny within our local church. Some people wondered whether it wasn't bad fruit from my leadership at home. I wondered about that as well. I didn't know what to think. Seeing what was happening with her older sister, our younger daughter's world then blew apart. She was misbehaving, adding more corroborating logs to the evidence of our family fire.

What did all of this mean? I had no idea. But a growing number of people assumed they did. We needed to do something.

The elders recommended an evaluation of my qualifications. I agreed. If that appears counterintuitive, one must appreciate the fierce scrutiny we were all under. We shared a collective desire to demonstrate our integrity, accountability, and transparency. It felt like an opportunity. I was also desperate to understand what I needed to learn from all of this.

The nine-month evaluation remains a blur. Eventually the elders reported the results to the church finding me imperfect but qualified for ministry. They also recommended I step away from my full-time role of serving the denomination to rejoin the pastoral team, stay local, and serve my family. This was really hard—I was still neck-deep in our denominational mess. But it seemed like folly to ignore the elders in this defining moment. With a heavy heart, I resigned.

In the months that followed there were many meetings, but little progress. The elders' evaluation had little impact upon the critics. Our family drama in the middle of the denominational debacle put our family under a brighter spotlight. Blogs were written, blame was spread, and criticism cut deep. As I think back, it's hard to capture the physical and mental depletion. Maybe you've been there; your life capsized by *defeated fatigue.*

Collateral damage continued. Kimm—my effervescent wife for over three decades—was emotionally tanking. My youngest daughter too. Locally, there was no role for me. Denominationally, there were no vacancies to fill in other churches. What was happening here? Everything I had spent my adult life building—home, church, job, friends—now seemed tenuous, up for grabs.

I waited for the bounce. You know, the divine reversal of fortune, the dramatic turn of events where the clouds break and the point behind it all crystallizes. But the bounce never came. The climate actually declined. The elders tried to help, but the momentum already underway created a tipping point. The unthinkable now seemed plausible. After three decades in our denomination and twenty-eight years in our local church, resignation seemed like the most reasonable option. We put our house on the market, stuffed the minivan to the roof, and left our home to start over in Florida.

I'll never forget careening down I-95 while Pink came on the radio singing about having scars on the heart, being broken, not bent, and learning to love again. A word in season. A tear streamed down my cheek.

That was twelve years ago.

A NEW CHAPTER MARKED BY MORE GRACE

How do I describe what has happened since then? The last decade has blended enduring grace with indescribable grief. We hoped the reset would help our youngest daughter. It did not. There was grace to fight alongside her until the day she passed. We miss her terribly.

We hoped that we could remain connected to our denomination. We could not. Invitations were canceled and many relational doors sealed shut. Three decades deleted.

Years passed. Grief over loss morphed into greater clarity over my own sin. Eventually, the peace known to those who "acknowledged that they were strangers and exiles on the earth" settled over my soul (Hebrews 11:13). Sightings of grace became more frequent. Grace to not oversimplify the complex. Grace to remember old friends for their best moments, just as we hoped they would do for us. Grace to concentrate more on the many good years than the few tragic ones. Grace to see that, in an imperfect world, God does not guarantee closure. Paul ended his life with deep relational disappointments. Most leaders will as well. Pity the pastor who needs closure to move forward. He is captive to the paralyzing idea that he is entitled to the benefits of heaven while still inhabiting earth.

In leaving those we loved, we hoped there would be fruitful ministry ahead. Thankfully, new doors opened wide and there was sufficient grace to limp forward. We were both sinners and sinned against. We love the church, despite her imperfections, just as we are loved.

Here we stand. Cracked clay pot and all.

MY HEART FOR YOUR SOUL

In the classic *Spiritual Leadership*, J. Oswald Sanders wrote, "A cross stands in the way of spiritual leadership, a cross upon which the leader must consent to be impaled."[5]

Ministry carries a paradox. Christians incite our greatest joys, but they also become the cross upon which we must consent to be impaled. We become the same for them. It's the irony behind ministry. We are called by God to love, nurture, and care for God's people—to invest our very lives in them—only to have our love misunderstood or unrequited. Or to have our own sins blunt the impact or intent of our friendship or service. And yet to move forward recognizing that this is all part of the call. We are called to serve the church without needing her approval. Pastoring is a deposit, not a transaction. We invest in the future of people, the church, and the kingdom, knowing one day the King will bring the return.

If we would lead God's people, we must resolve this in our heart: *To love the church is to become a target of her imperfections.* To bear the cross of leadership, we may become the object of appalling opposition or unrighteous behavior. "When unattached to the right ends," says David Brooks, "communities can be more barbarous than individuals."[6] Paul got it. When he said, "I endure everything for the sake of the elect" (2 Timothy 2:10), he had a large catalog of illustrations. Most pastors who finish well would say the same.

Yet even when she acts ugly, she is still Christ's bride. You must see her, not simply by how she fails but in light of who she is becoming (Ephesians 5:27). And from that glorious vision, you must be willing to bear the brokenness of the church to participate in God's work of reclamation. You must become, in the words of Andy Crouch, a "trustworthy trustee."

> It is amazing how consistently the stories of even the most complex institutions come down to their trustees, the ones who, at their best, bear the

institution's pain and brokenness, forgive it, and serve it. It is amazing how consistently the fate of institutions hinges on a few people, and their own personal character, how much even one person can tip the balance toward devastating injustice or toward redeeming abundance. And it is amazing how often the most trustworthy trustees are those who have personally experienced the worst that idolatry and injustice can do.[7]

It's hard to hear, I know. This trustee stuff requires some gracious grit. But that's your path—suffering with the church, sometimes *from* the church. You see, there was a clause in your call to ministry: an invitation to "share in suffering for the gospel by the power of God" (2 Timothy 1:8).

When Christ calls us to lead, it's not simply to herald the glorious gospel to other people. Pastoring becomes a merger between the message and ministry where the shepherd accepts the call to embody death and resurrection. "For we who are alive are always being given over to death for Jesus' sake, so that his life may also be revealed in our mortal body" (2 Corinthians 4:11 NIV). Ministry becomes a response to God's summons to reenact Christ's death and resurrection in our own life; to believe the gospel and become like the gospel; to "know

Him and the power of His resurrection and the fellowship of His sufferings, being conformed to His death" (Philippians 3:10 NASB).

Maybe you're reading this as a brokenhearted pastor. Your soul feels twisted over ways your clay pot was cracked. Looping through your mind is this message: *You're not enough. You're damaged goods. You'll never clear this hurdle of pain.* Maybe you are hurt, angry, or growing resentful over your impalement.

Here are five lessons I have learned to declutter the soul and make room for love.

LESSON # 1: KNOW YOUR LIMITS

You don't possess the power over others to produce the future you prefer or the change you would like to see. How others respond to you is beyond your control. Church imperfections—offenses, mistrust, betrayal (real or perceived), deep disappointments—these afflictions (from us and upon us) can burrow deep into the soul and occupy space unreachable to human effort. Only God works in that space. Only he can ultimately kindle the desire, adjust distorted ways of seeing and being seen, and transform people so that we can think differently. You are responsible only for your efforts toward others, the fruit of these efforts is up to God. Consider reading and rereading Matthew 5:2–24, Romans 12:18, and Hebrews 2:14, and ask the Spirit to sink these truths deep into your soul.

LESSON #2: KNOW YOUR ENEMY

Remember Satan? Well, he's real. And you are serving in a church situated on his turf. You think he's ambivalent about what you're up to? Not for a minute! Scripture calls him an "adversary" who "prowls around like a roaring lion, seeking someone to devour" (1 Peter 5:8). His food of choice is church leaders; his favorite dish is our faith.

In C. S. Lewis's classic *The Screwtape Letters*, the demonic mentor (Screwtape) advises his protégé (Wormwood) on how to discourage his Godward momentum. The secret strategy? *Disillusion the believer through the church.* "One of our greater allies at present," says Wormwood, "is the church itself." Screwtape tells Wormwood to help his subject see the commonness and hypocrisy in the church. "Work hard then on the disappointment or anticlimax which is certainly coming to the patient during his first weeks as a churchman."[8] Sadly, this strategy extends to leaders. *The church will disappoint you in ways that attack your faith to love and serve her.* Satan will exaggerate it. He'll try to punch the ignition on your resentment.

Satan loves to devour our awareness of God's existence and our anticipation that he is a "rewarder of those who seek Him" (Hebrews 11:6 LSB). By attacking our faith, Satan incubates doubt within the soul about God's work among God's people. It's for good reason Paul calls us to "Put on the whole armor of God, that you may be able to stand against the schemes of the devil" (Ephesians 6:11). An essential piece of that armor is "the shield of faith, with which you can extinguish all the flaming darts of the evil one" (Ephesians 6:16). If we want to finish the war without becoming casualties, we must use the shield. Thankfully faith is always given to those who ask. Keep asking, keep knocking. The Spirit will come into your heart and make his home with you as you make your home in him.

LESSON #3: KNOW YOUR GOD WHO STANDS BEHIND EVERY TROUBLE

Remember God's conspiracy. He is at work in your trouble, growing perseverance in the present and wonders for the future.

> So we do not lose heart. Though our outer self is wasting away, our inner self is being renewed day by day. For this light momentary affliction is

preparing for us an eternal weight of glory beyond all comparison, as we look not to the things that are seen but to the things that are unseen. For the things that are seen are transient, but the things that are unseen are eternal. (2 Corinthians 4:16–18)

Setbacks and failure can and do plague our leadership in this life. Progress with the church may be slow; sometimes even indiscernible. But we can persevere in confidence knowing that our field of labor is from God (2 Corinthians 4:1), good works have been prepared for us in this life (Ephesians 2:10), and wonders await us in the age to come (2 Corinthians 4:16–18).

Leaders, don't lose heart when setbacks come. Grieve your loss. Resist self-pity. Focus your faith. Embrace the call to suffer. Await the redemptive twist. *Remember the clay pot conspiracy.* God has promised to accomplish his purposes in you and through you. Sure, clouds of trouble may darken your life right now. But remember these lyrics to "God Moves in a Mysterious Way":

Ye fearful saints, fresh courage take;
The clouds ye so much dread
Are big with mercy and shall break
In blessings on your head.[9]

LESSON # 4: REMEMBER REDEMPTIVELY

A wounded heart does not traffic in nuance. It overgeneralizes. Creates caricatures. Recalls the ugly. Reduces people to their worst moments. *When we are hurt*, we can treat others in a way we would never want to be treated by God.

Think about how God has treated you. God takes our worst moments and announces that they are forgotten. He says, "I am he who blots out your transgressions for my own sake, and I will not remember your sins" (Isaiah 43:25).

You don't need the moral high ground; you need to remember the gospel—God saves sinners and that includes all of us. Keep in mind that you have done countless dumb and sinful things in life that are now covered over by God's unmerited favor. The more we truly understand grace, the more it tenderizes our heart. This makes it easier to remember people and ministries for their best moments (Psalm 103:12; Hebrews 8:12).

LESSON # 5: KNOW YOUR SHARED FUTURE

Broken connections can break hearts. They are some of the heaviest burdens we carry. Yet it is a temporary reality. A day is coming, and is not far off, when some Christians who might cross the street to avoid the awkwardness of greeting an estranged friend will weep for joy upon seeing the same person in the new heavens and new earth.

Remembering our shared future tempers our grievances. One day the hurt or anger that empowers our high-minded withdrawal or unforgiving disposition will be long forgotten. Instead, we will see surprising twists on how God used our scars to help us endure, to serve other sufferers, and to glorify God in ways we never dreamed. Here is what our future will be like with all God's people:

> And the ransomed of the LORD shall return
>   and come to Zion with singing;
> everlasting joy shall be upon their heads;
>   they shall obtain gladness and joy,
>   and sorrow and sighing shall flee away.
> (Isaiah 51:11)

LOVE NEVER FAILS

Leader, I wonder if it is time to reinterpret your story. *What if the pain you carry is an essential part of the call you answered? What if you really are on a journey toward coming to terms with your impalement? What if that pain is part of God's plan for your perseverance?*

God may be inviting you right now to remember the core of your call to Christ. "If anyone would come after me, let him deny himself and take up his cross and follow me" (Matthew 16:24). Yet the core of your call carries God's plan for your perseverance, "For you know that the testing of your faith produces steadfastness" (James 1:3).

God may be calling you to become a trustworthy trustee, to hear the summons from our Savior to stretch out your heart and consent to be impaled. Not because we glory in anguish, but because we finally comprehend that to love the church, we must come to terms with her imperfections.

While writing this book, we received an unexpected invitation from our old church to join them in celebrating their forty-year anniversary. We accepted. Kimm and I will soon travel to mark this moment with them—our first return since we departed over a decade ago.

I hope it goes well. I think it will. But really, it doesn't matter. Because the conspiracy carries an undeniable claim. We must be leaders who love, mirroring to each other how Jesus loves us. I think the invitation to return expresses that kind of desire from these church leaders.

But there's something else too. Waiting carries renewal. "They who wait for the LORD shall renew their strength" (Isaiah 40:31). Waiting runs steel rods through our resilience, strengthening the soul. Waiting deepens wonder because it slows us enough to see God's plan to convert death to resurrection life and use our pain—even church pain—to miraculously fortify our endurance. And that's a wonder we all need.

QUESTIONS FOR REFLECTION

1. Have you been wounded by the church? How can you trace the hand of God's grace through what happened? How might you apply the practice of "remembering redemptively" to this situation?
2. What changes might you need to make to become a more "trustworthy trustee"?
3. How would you retell portions of your life story or your ministry story if you were to interpret your pain as part of God's plan for your perseverance?

Wonder #5

REMEMBER GOD USES ENEMIES TO ENLARGE YOUR SOUL

Before you were a pastor, church leader, or a missionary, the idea of having enemies seemed theoretical; maybe even a bit antiquated. Who has actual enemies who want to destroy them in our day and age? But if becoming a Christian enlisted you into a cosmic war between good and evil, becoming a leader makes you an even larger target. In wonder #3, we looked at the enemy within us. But there is another enemy "prowling around like a roaring lion" seeking to devour your soul (1 Peter 5:8) There is also the "kosmos"—the world system—that hates you and is organized to oppose your progress (John 15:19). These spiritual realities are often embodied in real people—false leaders, false brethren, false teachers transmitting false doctrine—people with more charisma than character who create chaos that confuses Christians and depletes us.

No one advertises this, but leadership is a call to come under assault.

SETTING UP THE LAB

How does God shape us when we are under attack? It's a familiar question, though perhaps a bit clinical when posed in a book instead of in the middle of a battle. You know the right things to say; you've said them to others under attack. A slice of sovereignty, a pinch of promises, a splash of faith, all tossed together in a dish of God's goodness. It's a hearty meal you have fed to others. You know the ingredients. But now it's you. Your soul is starving and you have forgotten the recipe. You are feeling more than cracked—you fear that you are broken beyond repair.

How does grace meet a leader when our enemies cause a deep soul suffering? The right words don't seem to stick. But we repeat them, hoping repetition may supply what our soul needs. We still think pragmatically, as if this is about applying a formula, resolving a problem, or employing a strategy. We don't yet see it's about who we are becoming. An excavation has begun; the worksite is our life, the project our heart.

The last chapter unpacked how Christians can cause suffering for leaders and the amazing wonder that God uses those events to teach us about love and grace. My story had well-intended leaders seeking to navigate complexity and disagreement in principled ways. But there is another kind of assault on resilience which converts into our next wonder: the arrival of enemies.

God will use our enemies to uncover our idols. He will use foes to build our faith. We will learn to be kind to our enemies (Luke 6:35). It's hard to discern this wonder in the middle of the pain, but it's happening. *God is going to use your enemies to enlarge your soul.*

But first, who and what are our enemies? Is it only people? Scripture paints with broader strokes. Death, disease, depression—these too are enemies. Satan will use anything and anyone to try and destroy our faith. Perhaps your children have left home and faith, someone you love is struggling with an addiction, cancer is threatening you or someone you love, death has visited your family, a close friend has become a bitter critic— the list of enemies God's people face is long and varied. And yet the Spirit will not let your enemies destroy your faith.

The wonder is that God will use all of this to enlarge your soul. God will help you embody what you have said to others about grace and love.

STARTING THE LAB

To understand this wonder, you need to examine it. So, instead of just talking about it, let's begin the lab. Remember the high school science labs, where we donned goggles and aprons? The place where we prodded, mixed, experimented, detonated, and where some of us—well okay, maybe just me—almost flunked. The lab was where we pricked our fingers and looked at our blood under a microscope and dissected animal hearts—*real* hearts. Lab meant applying our knowledge. It meant surgery on frogs and pigs.

This chapter is a lab. So pick up your scalpel, and prepare to open your heart. You will need to peel back a few layers; it may draw blood. This probably seems untimely. But wounds are best tended when freshly inflicted. Take time right now to pray. God hears. He helps. He heals.

When we are attacked, how does God answer our prayers for help? How did he answer in the past? How about more recently? Think about this for a moment. Stop, ponder, and write down your answer here:

Perhaps one face, event, or circumstance popped immediately to mind, then that opened the yearbook to other faces, other trials, other pains. Maybe like David with Saul, your opposition was a family member who misunderstood and judged your motivations. Maybe it's someone you never met, but they have become experts on everything that is wrong with your church, your leadership, your ministry, your family. They ridicule, mock, blog; their questions are entrapments, their suggestions are slanders. Perhaps it's a disease or sinful obsession that took a family member or a marriage gone badly wrong.

How did you respond, or how are you responding right now? What marked you from the experience? If you trusted God, don't be afraid to say so. There's no humility in always assuming you failed. Christians believe in passing tests of faith (James 1:2–4). If you met something ugly from the world with something beautiful from God, be grateful.

But maybe you failed. If so, you're in good company. I've already described the season where it felt like ministry was imploding. It was an anxious, wearisome time. I've lost count of the ways I didn't trust God. Perhaps you can relate.

Open the mental file of your experience, put it on the screen. Now let's slide on the glasses of Psalm 56 and allow God's grace to focus what we see. God has launched a conspiracy. He is composing a song to reveal a wonder in his plan. Each stanza of the song is part of the wonder God wants your soul to learn.

STANZA ONE: TELL GOD HOW YOU FEEL

> Be gracious to me, O God, for man tramples on me;
> > all day long an attacker oppresses me;
> my enemies trample on me all day long,
> > for many attack me proudly. (vv. 1–2)

There was no "trampled-training" in seminary. It wasn't in any ministry job description. When we aspired to preach and serve God's people, we never dreamed our ministry, decisions, character, or family might become objects for soiled boots to trample. Ministry, we believed, is about bringing new life—conversions, change, church planting, good fruit, reconciliation, and new beginnings.

But "trampling"? No one said anything about trampling!

Sure, some opposition is no surprise. We studied the Gospels, the Corinthian corpus, the Judaizers, the Pharisees, Demas, and Alexander. We knew light could go dark, the world can take aim, we will be hated. Some opposition does not surprise us.

It's the duration. The unrelenting, faith-sapping, indefatigable, merciless, "all-day-longness" of the attack. "*All day long* an attacker oppresses me." "My enemies trample on me *all day long*." Ever felt that way? Not long ago I sought to hire a subcontractor. Word came back that he would not work with me. Slander from the past still lingered in the present. I thought the corner had been turned. But my life was still under his judgment.

This incessant trampling is no light bruising of the reed. It's more like reed-slaughter, aggravated reed-assault, reed-on-life-support. And maybe for you, it's not over. You're beginning to feel like your enemy's energy to destroy is more potent than your will to stand.

You're tired, and you're scared.

What becomes of a leader in the hands of prosecutors who operate with no mercy, no rules, no Bible? Where do we turn at such times? David prayed and told God exactly how he was feeling. And that's a good place to start. Perhaps this prayer of mine expresses some of what you are experiencing:

> Be gracious to me, O God. For I am suffering in ways unexpected and with a weariness that snuffs

out hope. Lord, I'm underwater, and fear floods my soul. I'm sure the trampling will eventually end, but what will be left of me? I'm confused, spent, frightened, embattled, and shredded by the relentless stomping of reckless foes. Be gracious to me, Lord, I won't make it without you!

Now you take a turn. Write out a prayer (here or in your journal) to tell God what you are feeling.

STANZA TWO: TELL GOD WHAT YOU FEAR

When I am afraid,
> I put my trust in you.

In God, whose word I praise,
> in God I trust; I shall not be afraid.

What can flesh do to me? (vv. 3–4)

King Saul had rallied the kingdom to pursue David. His crime? He was Saul's anointed successor. David represented the next generation of God's activity. But Saul would not relinquish the throne. He wanted to kill David.

Fear often lies, prophesying terrors that never materialize. But this is not that. David's fear was not irrational or exaggerated. This is not a molehill of hazard being fashioned into a mountain of life-threatening danger. No, Saul's sanity and thinking became so twisted that he saw David—his godly, loyal, courageous, son-in-law—as deserving immediate death.

Sometimes fear is entirely rational; it's the logical response to a credible threat. A sign that you are fully grasping the real danger. I've already described times when my life became even more painful than my worst fears could imagine. I remember thinking, with utter astonishment, that my dreadful imaginations of how bad things might get fell short. Life became so much worse. Those were days so dark and nights so void of hopeful signs that I felt abandoned by God.

David gets it. Threats of torture and demise are the backdrop of his hymn. What do you do when the only thing worse than the battle around you is the one within you? What did David do with his legitimate fears?

This is a lab, so answer it for yourself.

Now, what do you fear, can you name it? Be honest and specific—that fear does not define you, so saying it doesn't empower it. Equally important, we are unearthing God's wonderful conspiracy at work in your life.

Whatever fear you named, set it aside for a second. There's another important stanza to this hymn.

STANZA THREE: TELL YOUR SOUL ABOUT GRACE

> In God I trust; I shall not be afraid.
> What can flesh do to me? (v. 4)

It's not much. Just a faint ember sparking an intermittent glimmer from a dark corner of your soul. A grain of hope in the field of fear. A grace-shimmer, drawing your eyes away from the shadows and illuminating another presence, another power moving forward.

Grace is never passive. It arms you with questions: "What can flesh do to me?" Grace delivers reality by restoring God and people to their proper place.

Grace drills down to motives. "In what do I trust, right here, right now? Where is God in this story I'm telling myself?" Grace-infused questions, like a faithful sentry, halt our fear by checking its passport. "By what authority," grace investigates, "do you come to this mind with this message?"

REMEMBER GOD USES ENEMIES TO ENLARGE YOUR SOUL

Fear requires a passport to roam freely within our mind. What did you name? For fear to take root, you must first permit it safe passage to pillage your soul. But grace denies fear its passport, and instead turns and waves through God's promises.

Notice that David's mind is the first battlefield. When he is afraid, preoccupied, distracted, anxious, worried, bothered, nervous, fretting, besieged, how will he think? "I will put my trust in God." His situation has not changed. Saul is still crazy, and David's life is still threatened. But a monumental, life-transforming decision has been made. David will look to God despite his circumstances. He will trust God.

Sometimes we overspiritualize grace. We think grace invades the beaches of our fears with overwhelming firepower to liberate us from oppression. But grace is less like a tank division and more like a surgical strike. Grace spotlights God. It reaches past our fears, touches the chin, and tilts our gaze upward. Grace sparks faith, which fires our determination. This is what grace-fired determination sounds like:

- "I put my trust in you."
- "I have confidence in God, whose word I praise."
- "Fear will not own me. In God I trust!"

Grace engages reason. It seeks to unmask the irrationality of fear—even legitimate fears. Grace puts God and people in perspective. "What really can flesh do to me?" The question brings its answer along with it. "And do not fear those who kill the body but cannot kill the soul. Rather fear him who can destroy both soul and body in hell" (Matthew 10:28).

The clay pot conspiracy reminds us that our weakness is the staging ground for God's power. But to what end? For the wonder to work in the leader, yes—but grace goes further. The grace-filled, adversity-surrounded pastor looks through the pain and says, "It is all for your sake, so that as grace extends to more and more people it may increase thanksgiving, to the glory of God" (2 Corinthians 4:15).

Simple, yet eloquent; peaceful, yet potent; unassuming, yet undeniable; risky, yet unrelenting. That's the grace that fuels our trust.

STANZA FOUR - TELL YOUR SOUL THAT LEADERSHIP MEANS INJURY

All day long they injure my cause;
> all their thoughts are against me for evil.

They stir up strife, they lurk;
> they watch my steps,

as they have waited for my life.
   For their crime will they escape?
In wrath cast down the peoples, O God!
(Psalm 56:5–7)

Reckless, judgmental, cynical, divisive, suspicious—there are countless words for opponents who attack. David's descriptions share one diabolical denominator: *the intent to do evil.* The impact upon David's soul is painful and personal.

Few blows are more lethal to the leader's confidence than betrayal. For David, it was Saul—a patron who plucked him from obscurity and opened opportunities, his commander and king. Saul became suspicious, then seditious, then tragically sadistic. He wanted David dead.

Does a Saul have you in the crosshairs? A family member? A disgruntled group within your community? Someone who befriended you, enjoyed your gifts, knew your family, heard your hopes and dreams? But now everything has changed. They went dark, revised the history, made you the problem. Or maybe you've made real mistakes, but they are being blown way out of proportion. They are "injuring your cause," "stirring up strife," and "all their thoughts are against you for evil."

"For their crime will they escape?" You've asked the same question, maybe a dozen times. Maybe more. You're in good company. With David and with Jesus who also knew backstabbing—a close friend who shared meals with him and sold him out for a sack of silver (Psalm 41:9; Matthew 26:14–15).

Every wound you experience as you follow Jesus is an honor, an identification with him. When we suffer for our honest witness to and service for Christ, we can rejoice, because we know we are "filling up what is lacking in Christ's afflictions for the sake of his body, that is, the church" (Colossians 1:24). When we see this, we recognize the wonder—and it is *glorious*. Because God is not just providing hope in the midst of suffering; he's using your enemies to enlarge your soul—so that you become more like your faithful Savior Jesus.

STANZA FIVE: TELL YOUR SOUL GOD KNOWS

> You have kept count of my tossings;
> put my tears in your bottle.
> Are they not in your book? (Psalm 56:8)

The camera suddenly shifts from David's mind to God's heart and reveals a Lord who is there. Another sleepless night? The Maker is there counting tosses and turns. The tear-faucet won't shut off? Our Redeemer captures each one. Feeling alone and forgotten? Our Maker says, "There is not a single second where you have bled, or wept, or grieved, or cried out for relief that I don't enter into my book and remember for my purpose."

God understands. He knows the pain of having good deeds and intentions portrayed as evil. He knows that in a fallen world, things get flipped; he knows that by attacking you, people believe they are upholding truth and serving God's purpose. God knows!

Remember, this is a lab. Think about the person or people or circumstance you fear. Remember (and if you're married, remind your spouse), you are not the first person to have words distorted and motives dissected. Remember! You signed on to serve a Savior who was nailed to timber by those who thought they were serving God. Yet by submitting to this travesty, Christ redeemed us from our sin and now reminds us, *today*, "If anyone would come after me, let him deny himself and take up his cross daily and follow me" (Luke 9:23).

Do you remember how, as a new believer, you would ask God to make you like him, to help you make a radical difference in the world for Jesus?

This is how he is answering that prayer. Embrace the wonder.

STANZA SIX: TELL YOUR SOUL WHAT YOU KNOW

> Then my enemies will turn back
> in the day when I call.
> This I know, that God is for me.
> In God, whose word I praise,
> in the Lord, whose word I praise,
> in God I trust; I shall not be afraid.
> What can man do to me? (Psalm 56:9–11)

Faith is paradoxical. It demands our best thoughts in our worst moments. Faith calls us to God-exalting beliefs in earth-bound, soul-agonizing times. The key is where we flee when we fear. *This I know, that God is for me.*

Maybe your life is messy right now. Do you believe God is for you? I'm not asking if you feel it. The question is "Do you believe it?" God has paid the highest price to express his love and remove his opposition—he slaughtered his sinless Son to create an unbreakable connection with us. God does not withdraw his love when we falter or fail. He has fireproofed us against attack. "If God is for us, who can be against us?" (Romans 8:31).

But how do we fortify our confidence in God's unrelenting devotion to us?

David's confidence was connected to his practice of praising God's through his Word. To praise something is to value its worth. To value God's Word is to use it as a safehouse. It means elevating what God thinks about our suffering above what we think. When an anxious mind moves toward God's Word, faith stirs and grows.

Faith professes what it does not see (Hebrews 11:1). Faith detects heavenly realities in earthly rubble. To some people faith seems irrational, to others simpleminded. For David, it was the only way forward. So he kept on telling himself what he knew to be true: "When I call upon God, my enemies will turn back. God is for me; I don't need to be afraid. What can man do to me, I have God!"

This psalm teaches us to sing through suffering. In three different places, David praises God's Word as evidence of his trust (vv. 4a; 10a; 10b). He sings what is true until he feels what he sings. He praises what God said until he believes what God said.

Not long ago, this psalm blossomed with a fear-melting fragrance in a defining moment for me. One of my kids was not doing well. They were making choices that seemed to be moving them away from God. If you have ever walked this path with a child, you know the kind of soul-twisting anxiety it can incite.

As the worry raged, God led me to exchange my fretful thoughts with the words from Psalm 56. It wasn't easy. I can be pretty obsessive when I'm plowing my mental fields. But as fear filled my mind, I would set my mind instead on Psalm 56, reminding myself that "This I know, God is for me!" and "When I am afraid, I put my trust in you."

While my circumstances didn't change, the fear did. Praying God's Word weakened fear's grip. Thomas Chalmers called it "the expulsive power of a new affection." For us non-Puritans, think of it as the seatbelt strapping your soul to sanity. It's part of the journey toward deeper faith.

This is not some secret spell. We can be tempted when we feel attacked to downgrade God to a personal genie; just rub the bottle and wish adversity away. But God will not be bottled, yet his heart of love always moves his hand to give good things through hard times (Romans 8:28). David believed this. So he determined not to allow his enemy to dictate his response.

David sings before anything changes; and, this is so important, David sings even if nothing changes. This psalm sends us back to the lab to ask ourselves:

Does God need to change your situation to prove his love?

William Cowper said no. He composed "Welcome Cross," where the first verse confesses his confidence that God inscribes his love upon our trials.

> 'Tis my happiness below
> Not to live without the cross,
> But the Saviour's power to know,
> Sanctifying every loss;
> Trials must and will befall;
> But with humble faith to see
> Love inscribed upon them all,
> This is happiness to me.[1]

Job understood. He cried, "Though he slay me, I will hope in him" (13:15), while encountering inexplicable attacks, incalculable loss, and indescribable grief. His cry is a heart fighting for faith, a suffering soul that sings without holding God hostage for the change he desires. This song reminds us that because of Christ's fidelity to his promises, we can live with mystery. Our faith in God's love should not be based on feelings or circumstances; his love was decisively proven by our Savior's sacrificial death and victorious resurrection.

When we look at the cross, our tears and questions are answered.

It can be hard to access these truths when we are under attack. My first thought when enemies surround me is to sing of justice, vengeance, and self-pity. My songs often start and end with my own pain.

But David sings in another key. He's tuned to the Lord; he sings what God says. Then, slowly but surely, as the words of his praise penetrate his pain, hope happens. Paul reminds us that "hope does not disappoint" (Romans 5:5 NASB).

STANZA SEVEN - TELL YOUR SOUL TO RESPOND FAITHFULLY

> I must perform my vows to you, O God;
>   I will render thank offerings to you.
> For you have delivered my soul from death,
>   yes, my feet from falling,
> that I may walk before God
>   in the light of life. (Psalm 56:12–13)

God asks for our obedience even in our darkest moments, but he is not being cruel. What God commands is for our good. When, like David, we rise from our pain to "perform our vows" or "render thank offerings," we discover the surprising ways God is faithful to his Word. Desire is often reclaimed when we place actions before feelings. Spiritual progress materializes as we align our actions to God even when our circumstances seem unchanging. God is magnified as we respond faithfully and entrust ourselves to his lovingkindness.

In Numbers 17, Israel is surrounded by enemies and dying of thirst. God speaks to them saying, "Gather the people together, so that I may give them water" (Numbers 21:16). Then a funny thing happens: The people begin singing and digging. Deep into the burning sand they drive their tools until a faint gurgling sounds. Water is within reach. Responding faithfully to God's Word moves them forward, even while parched and surrounded by enemies! God is looking for faith from his people, and when you have faith, the Spirit helps you respond faithfully.

Back to the lab. What does it look like to "perform a vow," to respond faithfully to God with the fear you wrote down? Start by praying for the Spirit to bring what God would have you do into your mind. Maybe it means forgiving an enemy. Perhaps it's time to humble yourself and share your fears or pain to others. Perhaps you need to think less about the past and sing more in the present.

Suffering attack does not supply you with a special "get-out-of-jail" card to nurture bitterness or harbor anger toward anyone—including God. Returning evil for evil is not the way of God's people. Remember, we are never more vulnerable to the enemy or to our own desire for vindication than when we have been seriously sinned against.

Since this is a lab, spend some time thinking about how you have responded to your enemies' attacks. What do you see? It's easy to slowly assume a moral superiority through the power of a nurtured grievance. Sometimes it feels like the outrageous behavior of others should justify our resentment. I've been there. How about you? Have you been indulging your pain at the expense of your soul?

Our feet will never "walk before God in the light of life" if we walk that path. Rather, through suffering, we learn obedience (Hebrews 5:8). Obedience calls us to do what we don't desire so we can become who Christ has called us to be. That's how we are delivered over time. The defining moment arrives. We suffer, we obey, we die, we live. It's how we learn to "walk before God in the light of life."

SONG ENDED, LAB OVER, BACK TO LEADING

What have you learned about enduring attack? What do you now know about your opponent? What have you learned about yourself?

Hopefully, your gaze has shifted. You're neither looking inward nor pointing the finger out. It's no longer "Lord, what about them?" It's not even "Lord, what about me?" You're looking beyond people and beyond circumstances; God has grown bigger. It's now, "Lord, this is about you!"

No one wants to suffer. But no leader is spared this pain. For at the very intersection where your attacker meets your ministry, the lab ends and your soul is forged. It may feel excruciating. It may feel like your own, personal crucifixion. This is not an excuse to leave. It's an invitation to lean in, see God's wonders at work and anticipate a resurrection.

It's an opportunity to return to the heart of leadership: We are called to take up our cross, follow in the footsteps of our suffering, victorious Savior, and offer our clay pot as a receptacle for God's power. "But we have this treasure in jars of clay, to show that the surpassing power belongs to God and not to us" (2 Corinthians 4:7). When we suffer personally, privately, or publicly, we embody the sacrifice of Christ. We carry "in the body the death of Jesus, so that the life of Jesus may also be manifested in our bodies" (2 Corinthians 4:10).

When we are faithful and steadfast through pain, responding to adversity with a peaceful and kind spirit, overcoming evil with good and giving grace for slander, we testify that we embrace God's conspiracy and submit to his deep work. There is no alternative way to do ministry in the church. And there is no substitute for the glory it brings to our Lord.

Remember this wonder as you go back into the fire: God uses your enemies to enlarge your soul. So lean into the adversity. Your clay pot may feel busted, but Christ is at work in exceptional ways. Look up. Sing loud. Lead on.

QUESTIONS FOR REFLECTION

1. When was the last time you had an enemy? What did you fear? How did your fear reveal what you truly trust?
2. What are some of the key lessons you need to preach to your own soul when you feel under attack?
3. What are some practical ways you can respond to people who oppose you right now?

Wonder #6
BUILD STRONG TEAMS THROUGH WEAK LEADERS

One day in Caesarea Philippi, Jesus dropped a bomb on his team by announcing his impending death: "From that time Jesus began to show his disciples that he must go to Jerusalem and suffer many things from the elders and chief priests and scribes, and be killed, and on the third day be raised" (Matthew 16:21).

Never one to open his mouth without tasting a foot, Peter pulled Jesus aside for some life coaching, "Far be it from you, Lord! This shall never happen to you" (v. 22). If you preach, even occasionally, this should encourage you. Even Jesus had gospel messages that just didn't land. Knowing how much disciples needed repetition, he says it again in the next chapter (Matthew 17:22). But for Peter, this gospel seed found no purchase.

I can relate. As a new pastor, I saw Jesus in many glorious lights. But none of them really prioritized his death and resurrection. When I read this passage, I think of that young pastor spouting pious principles that were wholly disconnected from the central message of Scripture.

Remembering this makes me judge Peter less and identify with him more. His instincts here seem pretty rational. Peter's team leader—really, the all-time GOAT of team leaders—had just told his crew that he would suffer humiliation, torture, and death. Peter, thinking perhaps about this glorious ministry they are building, responds understandably: "God forbid!" He pleads with Jesus, "Lord, spare yourself this. We need you here. We need your gifts. The mission *needs you here*."

Then Jesus drops his infamous one-liner, "Get behind me, Satan!"

Think about this. What presents as a reasonable and caring response is actually a demonic temptation. Peter wanted to spare Jesus (and probably the team) from decline, weakness, and the suffering of the cross. But this was a cataclysmic blunder. Without the weakness of the cross, there would be no good news. Just imagine: no gospel hope, no local church, no church universal. No conversions, no transformation, no gospel mission. The irony here is the future turned on Jesus *not* listening to one of his closest friends.

REDEFINING EFFECTIVE TEAMS

Don't judge Peter too harshly. Or me. Peter speaks for us all. Like the disciples, ministry teams can also be tempted to overlook the conspiracy in the interest of progress. This looks like defining success without weakness, imagining mission without cost, pursuing godly leadership without gospel embodiment. This temptation to redefine the very essence of biblical success is frighteningly potent—especially for leaders.

As we have discussed, those of us in ministry naturally think we need to cover up our weaknesses and failures. All over the world, team cultures are developed so that strengths are celebrated over weaknesses, gifts are elevated over character, and statistical success is equated with ministry faithfulness. Leaders cultivate appetites for fast and famous fruit.

Zack Eswine is a pastor who understands. He said,

> As you enter ministry, you will be tempted to orient your desires toward doing large things in famous ways as fast and as efficiently as you can.

> But take note. A crossroads waits for you. Jesus is that crossroads. Because almost anything in life that truly matters will require you to do small, mostly overlooked things, over a long period of time with him. The pastoral vocation, because it focuses on helping people cultivate what truly matters, is therefore no exception.[1]

We've looked at how Paul learned this lesson. "Power," said Paul, "is made perfect in weakness" (2 Corinthians 12:9). This pathway is not merely a personal principle. It's also the key for cultivating a people and a place. An eldership, or any ministry team, flourishes as they understand and embody God's clay pot conspiracy. Because Christ's power inhabits teams who personify cross-shaped cultures. "For Christ's community to reflect his beauty," says Paul Miller, "Christian leaders need to constantly reenact his death."[2]

That's why this chapter's wonder is: *We build strong teams through weak leaders.*

How can this paradox be made practical? There are some actions we can take to help teams cultivate a culture of wise weakness. To build strong teams through weak leaders, we must aim for HEALTHY practices:

- **H**onor others
- **E**ncourage more than you want to be encouraged
- **A**cknowledge weaknesses more than parading strength
- **L**ook to the interests of others
- **T**alk less, and listen more
- **H**elp the weak
- **Y**earn for Christ

Let's unpack each of these points.

H—Honor others

Paul writes, "Outdo one another in showing honor" (Romans 12:10). What does honoring someone look and sound like? *Honor is openly voicing what we value.* When you enthusiastically tell your friends about a new sports documentary, or when your kid rocks a test and you shout, "I'm so proud of you," you're showing honor. In like manner, we give Jesus honor when we speak publicly about all that he means to us.

But how often does your church or ministry hear you give honor to the others around you? I'm not talking about the times we do this out of obligation or even when we spontaneously convey some form of vague praise. For honor to have impact, it must be specific. There's a huge difference between saying, "Ethan is a good marriage counselor," and adding more detail to your commendation with, "God has given Ethan wisdom to ask the right sort of questions, discernment to understand a person's heart, and clarity about how to apply the good news to broken marriages." For honor to truly land, it must find the runway of specificity.

Honor serves two purposes in growing us as leaders. First, it turns our attention away from ourselves toward others. In doing so, it weakens our self-infatuation and subverts our desire to grab glory. It's not an exaggeration to say that honoring the qualities of others can help weaken the grip of our own natural self-centeredness.

Second, it presses us to study those we serve so we can find things in their lives to celebrate. We can then skillfully praise the words and works of others. Such gestures, though brief, become the building blocks through which team cultures are constructed.

Make it your practice to study others—beginning with your spouse—so you can really understand their strengths. Then, as your focus sharpens, show honor by giving voice to what you value. If you lead a team, make this a part of your regular preparation for team meetings. Learn to mark those moments together by practicing godly affirmation. Aim for a culture where the team does it naturally and frequently. You'll know you are getting close when the practice begins to happen even when it is not on the agenda.

Even in the midst of suffering, King David found joy in the people God placed around him. He writes, "As for the saints in the land, they are the excellent ones, in whom is all my delight" (Psalm 16:3). David found delight in the excellence of other saints. This passage reminds me of something I read about George Whitefield. After his death, a friend made a keen observation after reading his journals, "In [Whitefield's] journals and letters, an impartial reader will find instances thereof almost in every page: such as, lively gratitude to God in the first place, and to all whom God had used as instruments of good to him."[3]

Think about giving honor in Whitefield's way—offering lively public gratitude for all whom God has used as instruments of good to you. Ask yourself, *Am I known as a team member who offers lively public gratitude for those around me?*

Here's another way to connect honor, team cultures, and wise weakness: Wherever possible, underscore your dependence upon others. For instance, learn to tell your leadership journey as a testimony about the others who have influenced your life. You'll be surprised by the number of heroes in your story. After all, Christian leaders are not parachuted from heaven into roles. We are an ongoing community project. Do you remember the people who helped to shape your leadership? Make public declarations that your ministry is not about the genius of one (you) but rather about the faithfulness of many upon whose shoulders you stand.

Proud leaders have trouble doing this. Apart from grace, we can feel strong cravings to create narratives where other people only played small supporting roles in how we were shaped. We are drawn to origin stories that put ourselves at the center and minimize the influence of others. We edit out the contributions of others of our story or just portray our growth as if it comes only from our deep engagement with God and the Bible. It's subtle, and often done eloquently. But it's sanitized from all earthly influences who could legitimately be honored.

Pride distorts our personal biographies. It convinces us that we became an effective leader independently—powered by our own gifts, abilities, and prowess. As a result, people only see a greater and stronger leader. "*Wow, look at him—God alone has shaped him!*" But this is never true. That kind of leader has just conveniently forgotten a whole lot of influences along the way. And he grows proud and vulnerable trying to appear like the genius who descended from his mountain meetings with God.

"God is glorified in us," says Sam Crabtree, "when we affirm the work he has done and is doing in others."[4] Ask yourself right now, *Am I known as a leader who knows the importance of others' contributions? Am I known as a leader that knows his need for others?* Then—if you really want to test your answers—ask your wife and your team.

E—Encourage others more than you seek encouragement

If honor is public praise, then encouragement is private inspiration.

Do you want to know something fascinating about humans? God has framed us in such a way that people's words matter. We can be inspired by speeches. We have our imaginations stoked through well-timed words. Think of Churchill lifting the vision of England during the war through the power of his radio addresses. We can also be admonished by loving rebuke and refreshed by a well-chosen turn of phrase. As Proverbs teach us, "A word fitly spoken is like apples of gold in a setting of silver" (25:11). Words can sting us, or they can help us soar. They can be wise, or weaponized.

Here's my point. Words inspire godly action. So, God tells us to "consider how to stir up one another to love and good works" (Hebrews 10:24). And also to "encourage one another and build one another up, just as you are doing" (1 Thessalonians 5:11).

Our role as church leaders is to create a team culture that models passages like this—one that exhibits and embodies these encouraging words. Every leader wants to be *in* that culture, but the best leaders will want to know how to build it. Encouragement reminds us that words build teams. Teams then become ecosystems that influence the health of the church.[5]

But we don't build encouragement by demanding it of others. If you want a team that expresses encouragement, start to encourage. Cultures are built through modeling and practice. This starts with team leaders but includes each member too. Cultures of encouragement emerge by applying the golden rule: we encourage others as we would want them to encourage us. Build the Bible into how you encourage too. Let people know how you see them embodying passages and principles from Scripture.

Over time, individual gestures of appreciation and value become postures. Can you see how it works? For teams to become strong in giving encouragement, you must become their encouraging servant.

A—Acknowledge weakness more than parading strengths

We've already learned about the context behind Paul's writing of 2 Corinthians. There was great turmoil. Detractors were planning a coup in the Corinthian church. The goal was to subvert Paul and seduce the church into following their leadership. Do you remember what Paul did? He defended himself by acknowledging his weaknesses as a way to glorify God and portray the conspiracy.

People tend to assume that their leaders are strong. We've got a microphone, gifting, and a story about being called by the Creator of the Universe. If we use that microphone to remind people of our strengths, make ourselves the hero of the story, share illustrations that make us look strong, or confess problems that are always resolved, people may admire us. But they can't relate to us. They may respect us, but they won't come to us. "The lesson," says Arthur Brooks, "is that if you want to make a deep human connection with someone, your strengths and worldly successes won't cut it. You need your weaknesses for that."[6]

The clay pot is a connecting point. Weaknesses level the playing field. Like Paul, we should put our weak foot forward, and we should be honest about our struggles. If you've recently received some helpful correction (or even unhelpful criticism), tell your team about it. Sure, as we discussed, leaders can be manipulatively vulnerable, overshare, or use personal vulnerability as a currency to purchase favor. No confession is flawless. But it's better to aim for honest confession. You'll know it's honest when it makes you look not strong, but vulnerable. The conspiracy reminds us that what feels weak can be good. It shows your team members that you are an imperfect leader.

Acknowledging weakness includes fostering a culture where there is freedom to confess our sins to one another (James 5:16). Don't we all know we are sinners? Why not just eliminate the curiosity over how it happens through confession! Without free confession, we drift toward what John Piper calls, "naive admiration," producing a bubble where leaders become symbolic and appear unrelatable. Bubbles, however, are fragile and burst easily. Admiration-driven team systems that produce hero worship have thin membranes. When weaknesses or sins are revealed, team bubbles are punctured and leave everyone feeling defrauded. Piper's full quote is, "Disillusionment often follows naive admiration."[7]

Without a culture of confession, pastors become holy artifacts admired by people from afar, like relics nestled in the Vatican. That is, of course, until it becomes evident that the pastor is just as much a sinner as every other person. Part of the reason people become disillusioned and disenchanted is that the leaders they once admired fail to live up to uninformed expectations. Wise leaders inform wisely.

For your team to be strong, you must boast appropriately about your weaknesses and avoid parading your strengths. I'm not advising you to ignore or deny them. Just cancel the parade.

L—Look to the interests of others

Philippians 2:4 says, "Let each of you look not only to his own interests, but also to the interests of others." Just to be clear, this passage doesn't call for detached selflessness. Rather, the passage can also be translated, "Do not merely look out for your own personal interests" (NASB). *Merely* looking out for yourself is worldly. We must add living to make others successful.

God provides a clue in verse 4 about how to measure how we're doing with this. Take the passion and concern you have for your own interests (or agenda) and use that as the standard to measure the passion you bring to the agenda of others. In other words, serve the others on the team the way you would want to be served.

If you lead a team, ask yourself, *Does our team know that I am out for their best interests? Do they believe that their souls and their physical health are more important to me than what they can accomplish in ministry? Do they know that I will make sacrifices for them? Do they know they can be vulnerable with me and not have it used against them? Do they know that I would reconsider my role for the good of the church? Are they confident that, in the right timing, I want to entrust responsibility to them? Would I be known as someone who, when necessary, apologizes?*

Let me tell you about a time I failed at this. A team member was doing a message on elders and, in moment of wanting to look out for his interests (or so I thought), I offered him some material from a book I was about to publish. But when I eventually saw his notes, I realized that he was diving deeper into the materials than I expected. No plagiarism, mind you, and he was clearly crediting me. But somehow that was no longer enough. I started to feel territorial and flagged him for how much of the material he was using. The material, that is, that I gave him to use!

Fierce self-interest. It's the addiction that makes me appear both small *and* stupid.

By God's grace, I was convicted. My territorial heart wasn't about his interests at all. It was the Me-Dragon that lives to protect the cave of *my own* interests. The only reason I'm not toxically selfish is because of the gospel. My hope is not in the purity of my motives, but in the purity of Christ's motives. The gospel is the glorious reminder that all my sinful interest grubbing was laid upon the One who always had the honor of God in view. Therefore, I can trust in the Savior even when my heart drifts toward myself.

Here's one more application of this point. Churches will never be planted unless we're willing to act in the best interest of the planter and the lost who are not yet formed into churches. We need to see that the Great Commission is one of the best applications of Philippians 2:4. Christ's commission at the end of Matthew calls us to train and send out good people for kingdom benefits. As we do so, we display our commitment to the interests of others—and enjoy the blessing of being part of God's larger plan for bringing the gospel to the whole world.

Practically this means that we keep pushing some of our best and brightest people out the door and off into gospel work. We do so because we are willing to look also to the interests of the kingdom, not just the interests of our local church. "Sending means giving away some of your best leaders and letting go of needed resources. It means giving away opportunities in the kingdom, and watching others get credit for successes that you could easily have obtained for yourself. The only way you'll be willing to do that is if you love Jesus's kingdom more than your own."[8]

For the mission to be strong, we must embrace sacrifice. We must practice *healthy* weakness.

T—Talk less, and listen more

This is a hard one for people who make their living through talking—a lot—but James 1:19 says, "Let every person be quick to hear, slow to speak, slow to anger." Ask yourself, *Do people experience me as quick to hear and slow to speak? Are you quick to provide answers? Quick to express opinions? Quick to talk over others? Quick to want to display insight or intellect? Quick to diagnose?* I've done all of that. Typically, it's a way for me to appear strong, to impress other people.

If you are on a team, ask yourself: *Does our communication culture follow the James 1:19 model? Or do we roll more with the inverted version of this passage, "quick to speak, slow to listen"? Do people love others more and the church more because of the way they hear our team talk about each other?* "Out of the abundance of the heart the mouth speaks" (Luke 6:45). *What does our speech say about what we really value as a team?*

The beauty of the gospel is that it shapes our identity; it speaks over us and for us so that we no longer need to be speaking words from posturing or self-protection. As a leader applies the gospel, he becomes more secure. Envy erodes. Talking decreases, curiosity is sparked, listening grows. He doesn't give up leadership. He just sees ways to influence beyond his word count.

The wise pastor knows that his personality will surface even in his silence. He could hold court in an elder meeting but instead he talks less and asks a lot of questions. Jonathan Leeman of 9Marks wrote a helpful article about his boss, entitled "How Mark Dever Passes Out Authority."[9] He described how Pastor Dever is constantly presented with the opportunity to accrue more authority, but he gives most of it away. Dever, he says, first builds the ministry with his elder team. He limits his preaching slots to 50 to 60 percent of the time, which, as an aside, can be a revealing window into the preacher's security and commitment to train other expositors. According to Leeman, Dever lets others use his ideas. He speaks sparingly at elder meetings; he doesn't even chair them. He invites criticism from members of the congregation.

Leeman spends the second half of the article describing how this leadership model has profoundly influenced the culture of Dever's church. Chief among these are the ways that this culture destroys natural social hierarchies and cultivates a willingness to forgive.

As I read this article, it occurred to me that Dever's self-emptying has impacted his church to such a degree that he is actually valued more. So the fears that underlie our many words and our reticence to give away power—*I'll be forgotten; I'll be taken advantage of; I'll become useless*—wither like weeds under the heat of gospel truth.

When Christ emptied himself of power, he was exalted (Philippians 2:6–9). After death comes resurrection. It's a gospel principle. We are blessed by following in Jesus's steps, even if that honor only comes when we hear God's words, "Well done good and faithful servant," as we enter heaven (Matthew 25:23).

H—Help the weak

First Thessalonians 5:14 says, "And we urge you, brothers, admonish the idle, encourage the fainthearted, help the weak, be patient with them all." Weakness is the humbled condition that unlocks all the wonders within the conspiracy, but here it is portrayed as an identifiable group. "The weak" are those who need support or assistance because they are struggling and vulnerable. We've all been there.

Sometimes, in fact, we are "the weak" because we share similar weaknesses. Maybe its aging, brain chemistry, autism, addiction, depression, or disease. Perhaps it's our mistakes—the lights left on, the dented fenders, the dumb things we say, or poor choices with our money. Nobody's sinning. We're just human, imperfect, and limited. We are not omnipotent, omniscient, or omnicompetent. In other words, we're not God.

BUILD STRONG TEAMS THROUGH WEAK LEADERS

Teams are a collective of the weak. How we respond when those weaknesses surface will determine the culture we build and transfer. I once spent a lot of money producing a product for our ministry that was, well, to put it delicately, *underwhelming*. An indelicate voice might say that it was a decent idea executed stupidly and expensively, ultimately rendering it unusable.

But the response was not the obvious one ("What were you thinking!"), instead my effort was praised and intentions were ennobled. I was never made to feel stupid. Those around me chose to believe the best of me. My weakness did not define me. It was grace. Only grace. The kind that quickly moves you beyond the strikeout and makes you want to bat again. To swing again. To stay in the game. Keep innovating. It also made me want to pass along to others the same patience I had received.

Each person's struggle requires a unique response—admonishment, encouragement, and help. The best leaders will know how to distinguish between the team member who is idle, one who is fainthearted, and one who is simply weak. But it's interesting where Paul ends. He says, "Be patient with them all."

We can be patient with a team member even when we don't approve of their performance. Performance is not irrelevant, it's only that your ability to honor their personhood and uphold their dignity is not tied to their performance. We can respect and accept them even while we expect change. We can call for growth in excellence without withdrawing approval or adjusting our relationship with them. We can also let them go because we have helped them see that their gifts will flourish more in another role.

Patience means we don't punish people who disappoint us. We don't demean them with words or toss them to the sidelines. There's no ghosting; there's no icing them out because they did not meet our expectations. A gospel culture guides our team whether we are hiring, reviewing, or firing.

Remember, we didn't hire Jesus. We hired fallen human beings with strengths and *weaknesses*. How we relate to those weaknesses will create a culture. The only question is whether it will be fragrant with the gospel or default toward pragmatism or legalism. Wise team leaders and members will relate to others with the same patience we want to be given. Because—just like everyone else—we are *weak*.

Y—Yearn for the Savior

We don't honor others, encourage, acknowledge weaknesses, look to others' interests, talk less, and help the weak simply because it's a good team-building tactic or just to get better results. This is not a transaction we make with the team for higher performance. No, the gospel empowers our leadership. Second Corinthians 13:4 says it this way, "For he was crucified in weakness, but lives by the power of God. For we also are weak in him, but in dealing with you we will live with him by the power of God."

The center of our faith and the secret of our impact are the same. God conquered the sins and failings of humanity through the weakness of the cross, and God has ordained that our weakness be the connecting point for powerful transforming grace. The cross vanquishes our trust in human ability by exposing the folly of human wisdom and strength.

No one comes to know God by human strength and wisdom but rather by faith alone (1 Corinthians 1:20–21). This is offensive and confounding to a world that boasts of human strength and depends upon performance. But for the humble and weak, this message is powerful. Because it's at the point of our own *inability* where we experience the transforming power of God.

We need teams that get this right, teams that understand the secret of leadership is the way of the cross. We need men who, like Paul, "know nothing among you except for Jesus Christ and him crucified" (1 Corinthians 2:2). We need men who can follow Christ by being crucified in weakness so that they can live in power. We need team cultures that understand and celebrate the clay pot conspiracy.

Like Peter in Matthew 16, our temptation is to define success without weakness, to cover up our weaknesses and failures. But the cross shows us that for the church to be strong, we must become weak. So we don't lead and love our teams in merely convenient ways. We strive to be *H-E-A-L-T-H-Y.* Because we know the strongest teams are populated by weak leaders encountering the power of God.

QUESTIONS FOR REFLECTION

1. Think back to when you first entered ministry. What was your idea of effective leadership? How does the call to reenact the gospel help change your definition of leadership?
2. How have others helped you on your ministry or leadership journey? Be specific. Then thank God for them.
3. Which HEALTHY practices come most naturally to you? Which of the practices call you to greater growth?

Wonder #7
RUN TOGETHER TO FINISH WELL

We've journeyed a long way together to unravel the clay pot conspiracy. We have beheld six glorious wonders that catalyze power and resilience, where the updraft of God's grace meet the downdraft of our weakness. Ministry becomes charged; lightning strikes clay; faith ignites; resilience is fortified. Fresh desires are kindled to stand firm, lead forward, and resist weariness—all playing a part in empowering us to finish well our dangerous journey.

One wonder awaits. A surprising twist tucked into the ending of the classic allegory *The Pilgrim's Progress*. Behold with me the wonder of finishing the race together.

THE BROKEN YET BUOYANT BUNYAN

Bunyan writes as an embattled pastor in a broken world. He grew up in poverty. His first wife died less than a decade after they married, and he was left with four children; Mary, his oldest, was born blind. A single parent, living in poverty, working at the trade of mending utensils while raising four kids—that was Bunyan's world.

During his first marriage, John Bunyan was converted and called to preach. His ministry reenacted the humiliation—and, eventually, the glory—of the gospel. Bunyan's family, his past, and his suffering created burdens and baggage. He experienced mental and emotional turmoil. He also experienced attacks from the devil, who would tempt him to abandon Christ. Once he did walk away, only to discover Christ had not abandoned him.[1]

When Bunyan began to preach, he was slandered and maligned due to his lack of formal education. His ministry and intelligence were insulted. He cared for a special-needs child, suffered as his second wife miscarried, and, then finally endured an infamous imprisonment. No one had to convince John Bunyan that ministry meant suffering. His trials were his tutor. Jacob Tanner observes that "It was, perhaps, this firsthand experience with persecution and suffering that made Bunyan's writings and preaching so impactful and visceral to his readers and listeners. This was not a man merely engaged in thinking about suffering, but a man of God who had gone through the furnace."[2] John Bunyan became well acquainted with his fragile clay pot, its troubling cracks, and God's wondrous conspiracy to fill our weakness with his grace.

For Bunyan, *Pilgrim's Progress* forms a kind of allegorical autobiography. The dangers, toils, and snares that the main character, Christian, encounters mirror many of Bunyan's experiences. Referencing the literary characters in his book, another biographer observes, "They are not fancy pictures, but literal portraits. . . . His bold personifications are truthfully drawn from his own experience. . . . He could have given a personal name to most of them." Describing his emotional and ministry suffering, the biographer continues, "He had known what it was to be in danger of falling into a pit and being dashed to pieces with Vain Confidence, of being drowned in the flooded meadows with Christian and Hopeful; of sinking in deep water when swimming over a river, going down and rising up half dead, and needing all his companion's strength and skill to keep his head above the stream."[3]

Here's my point: Bunyan, a pastor acquainted with grief and suffering, must have certainly wrote the end of his book with the end of his own life in mind. To a question—"how can I finish well?"—stamped upon the mind of so many in ministry, we might take this final scene as the answer from a brother pastor, seasoned in the seminary of suffering. Our final wonder surfaces most clearly through Bunyan's vision of the climactic death-scene, where Christian and Hopeful crossed the river.

RUN TOGETHER TO FINISH WELL

As an allegory for dying, this is a gripping scene. Christian arrived at the river of Death after an arduous journey. He was caught in the Slough of Despond and imprisoned in Doubting Castle; he quaked before the Giant Despair, navigated the treacheries of Vanity Fair, suffered wounds from the blows of Apollyon, and negotiated a cast of characters often urging him to leave God's path for an easier journey. Yet he kept the faith.

Finally, his perilous expedition neared completion. Christian faced the final obstacle before the Celestial City. Yet here Bunyan swerved. The river crossing was not a triumphant celebration through the passage of death. Christian was not filled with faith to advance victoriously toward his final conquest. It was just the opposite.

Christian stood embattled, his body scarred, his wounds deep. His confidence wavered. Christian's clay pot seemed not just broken, but unsalvageable. In this final moment when we expect to see the adrenaline surge to get him across the finish line, Christian stumbled and fell, all within a few steps of heaven's gate.

Bunyan told the story:

> They went on together until they came in sight of the Gate.
>
> Between them and the Gate was a River, but there was no Bridge to go over the River and the River was very deep. At the sight of the River the Pilgrims were stunned, but the men with them said, "You must go through the River or you cannot come at the Gate.
>
> The Pilgrims then, especially Christian, began to despair in his mind. He looked every which way, but could not find any other way to go to escape the River. They asked the men if the Waters were all the same depth? They answered, no, but they could not help them find out where it was easier. They said, "You shall find it deeper or shallower, depending on your faith in the King of the place."
>
> And so they turned themselves to the Water, and entering, Christian began to sink. He cried out to his good friend, Hopeful, and said, "I sink in deep Waters; the Billows go over my head, all his Waves go over me, Selah."[4]

Ending well means dying well. John Wesley once said of his congregation, "Our people die well." For Wesley, dying well was evidence of living faithfully toward God.

I'm not disputing Wesley's claim. Nor, may I add, do I desire to go to heaven in any way but "well." Dying "ugly" raises suspicions about your running. Is some undisclosed sin sneaking up on the conscience? Some last-minute stumbling can be so bad that we question whether the runner is even in the right race. Recently, I heard a story where a widely respected gospel preacher was trying to make sense of his mentor's erratic behavior as he died. The mentor's passing was something akin to *kicking and screaming through despair*.

Nobody wants that. We want the D. L. Moody option: "Earth recedes, heavens open before me. If this is death, it is sweet. There is no valley here. God is calling me, and I must go."[5]

Sign me up for the Moody crossing. I'll take a bridge over the water—better yet, a yacht. At a minimum, can I see a package that includes snorkel gear?

What was Bunyan thinking? He was a pastor. He knew we feel deeply responsible to lead wisely and die well. He understood the need to help believers die well. Why paint such a troubled picture?

Bunyan wanted a different ending. Perhaps he was making a different point.

HOPEFUL COMFORTS

Then Hopeful replied, "Take courage, my brother—I feel the bottom, and it is firm!"

Christian then cried out, "Ah! my friend, the sorrows of death have compassed me about! I shall not see the land which flows with milk and honey!" With that, a great darkness and horror fell upon Christian, so that he could not see ahead of him. He also, in great measure, lost his senses—so that he could neither remember, nor talk coherently of any of those sweet refreshments which he had met with along the way of his pilgrimage. But all the words that he spoke still tended to manifest his horror of mind and heart-fears—that he would die in that river, and never obtain entrance at the gate.

Hopeful, therefore, labored hard to keep his brother's head above water. Yes, sometimes Christian almost drowned—but then, in a short time, he would surface again, half dead. Hopeful would also endeavor to encourage him, saying, "Brother, I see the gate—and men standing ready to receive us!"

But Christian would answer, "It is you—it is you they are waiting for! You have been Hopeful ever since I first knew you!"

> "And so have you," responded Hopeful.
>
> "Ah, brother!" cried Christian, "Surely if I were right with Him—then He would now arise to help me. Because of my sins, He has brought me into the snare, and has left me."[6]

The further he went across the river, the more questions I have. Do you wonder about your own passing? What would we see if we glimpsed our own clay pot's final moments? A vision of a mighty victor? A spiritual giant forging a path through the waves? Maybe. I hope so. But Bunyan showed us something else. I think he wanted us to see Christian's clay pot—even as he stepped out of the shadowlands and crossed through the river.

Christian was not crossing as a spiritual superstar or surfing across and sliding resplendently into heaven. Christian was dying as an embattled soldier—a wounded warrior with feeble faith, struggling. It's a surprising and sober scene. Christian is not simply weak—his faith is failing. He touches despair.

I think Bunyan's portrayal was a stroke of genius. Christian died just as he lived—as a clay pot, filled with treasure, but cracked by his journey through a broken world. Christian was never a stunning specimen of determined law-keeping. He lived as a traveler who was prone to wander off God's path. A sinner growing more aware of his sinfulness. Stumbling forward, unable to shake his weaknesses. He's me. And you. Desperate for progress, yet constantly needing outside intervention.

Bunyan wanted us to see this: Christian wandered, but *he was never alone.*

I don't think we are meant to overanalyze Christian's faltering faith. Many Christians will die confident, fixing their eyes upon the destination. But some will tremble forward in fear until they are safely home. Our confidence in passing, according to Bunyan, will be proportional to our faith: "You shall find it deeper or shallower, depending on your faith in the King of the place."

But this is where Bunyan inserts the wonder. Christian did not journey alone. Crossing alongside him was Hopeful—his friend for the final leg of his journey. The man symbolizes a long line of people who helped Christian along the way, but he was by far the most consequential. For in the darkest moments of Christian's life, he had a friend who inspired his faith toward God.

Faith is a paradox. As Hebrews 11:1 states, "Faith is the assurance of things hoped for, the conviction of things not seen." Our foundation is firm and unshakable, but it is also invisible and not yet realized. There is another paradox. Faith is individual; Scripture warns us, "If you do not stand firm in your faith, you will not stand at all" (Isaiah 7:9 NIV). Yet, faith is also communal; Ecclesiastes tells us that there is strength in numbers (4:12). While we each must stand firm in our own faith, the Lord ordains brothers to help us find our feet. Exhibit A: Hopeful.

HOPEFUL SPEAKS AGAIN

> Then Hopeful said, "My Brother, you have forgotten the Text where it is said of the wicked: 'There is no band in their death, but their strength is firm, they are not troubled as other men, neither are they plagued like other men.' These troubles and distresses that you go through in these waters are not a sign that God has forsaken you, but they are sent to test you, to see whether you will remember how you have lived because of his goodness, and live still upon them in your distresses."
>
> Christian fell into thought for a while and so Hopeful added these words, "Be of good cheer, Jesus Christ makes you whole!" With those words, Christian broke out into a loud voice, "Oh, I see him again, and he is telling me, 'When you pass through the Waters, I will be with you, and the Rivers will not overflow you.'"

> Then both of the Pilgrims had courage. . . . Christian soon found ground to stand on in the River and the rest of the way was shallow, and they got over.[7]

Do you see what happens? When Christian sunk, Hopeful stood. When Christian was fearful, Hopeful stirred faith. Bunyan showed us how grace flowed through Hopeful. We are impressed by one gripping truth: *Christian finished the race because he did not run it alone.* This is a wonder.

Paul exhorts us in one place to run like the Olympic athletes—and "only one receives the prize!" (1 Corinthians 9:24). That is reasonable and, if you're at all competitive, attractive too. But the wonder of running the race together is that the crown we win is not at the expense of the other brothers. Rather, our crown is the other brothers (Philippians 4:1; 1 Thessalonians 2:19).

Charles Spurgeon once said, "He who is his own guide is guided by a fool."[8] Certainly there were times when Christian was alone. But his story is one where God brought guides and Christian took notes. If you've read *Pilgrim's Progress*, you are acquainted with the cast of sages, encouragers, and coaches he encounters along the way: Evangelist, Help, Mr. Great-Heart, Discretion,

Piety, Prudence, Charity, Faithful, The Interpreter, and of course Hopeful.

Christian was not his own guide. Bunyan was so intent on the point that he writes the river scene with two people crossing (or dying) simultaneously. Because of Hopeful, Christian finishes the race. When Christian's faith was absent, a hopeful friend was present.

Companionship, community, plurality—these are unexpected wonders in Christian's story. The friends who accompanied him along the way supported him, exhorted him, spoke truth to his doubts, and inspired his faith when it seems lost. Hopeful symbolizes the wonder of genuine comrades, who personify grace and courage when we need it the most. These are the friends who love us enough to spare no effort, no sacrifice, and no expense to keep our head above the water. Those who call us to stand our ground, look beyond the waves to the Savior and finish the race set before us. To know even one is to experience a sweet mercy from God. Richard Baxter said, "It is a mercy to have a faithful friend that loveth you entirely . . . to whom you may open your mind and communicate your affairs. . . . And it is a mercy to have so near a friend to be a helper to your soul and . . . to stir up in you the grace of God."[9]

ON BECOMING HOPEFUL

How can we find true-hearted gospel partners like that? We all want friends who are willing to cross treacherous channels riding shotgun. We long for companions who have our back, speak faith to our doubt, and will, when necessary, drag us forward when we can go no further. "Come, Mr. Frodo! I can't carry it for you, but I can carry you!"[10] The giant-hearted Samwise Gamgee was Tolkien's version of Hopeful: *The friend God uses to bear our burden and help us finish well.*

If you're finishing this book with no Hopeful in sight, let me supply a fixed point from which you can plot your direction and navigate your journey.

BECOME THE HOPEFUL YOU WANT TO ATTRACT

Finding Hopeful is not first about looking, but about becoming. Become the friend you would most desire to accompany you. With magnets, opposites attract. But with Hopeful-leaders, like attracts like. Courage begets courage. Vision attracts visionaries. Noble souls draw others who aspire to become large-souled.

What we embody, we attract.

To draw the caliber of Hopeful, you must be Hopeful to others. "So whatever you wish that others would do to you, do also to them" (Matthew 7:12).

What does it look like to "do also to them"? Here are ten ways to become the kind of leader that first models, then gathers Hopefuls.

1. *Seek to sympathize.* To draw good friends, leaders must be tender-hearted. When you notice weaknesses surfacing in others, respond with sympathy. You can quickly identify with human weakness because you live with an awareness of your own. During the crossing, Christian's weakness and stumbling became an opportunity for Hopeful to provide ministry. Rather than conveying moral superiority or disapproval, Hopeful carried Christian and inspired him to keep looking toward God. In doing so, he reflected the heart of our gentle Savior who, despite being sinless and morally perfect, has kind and loving sympathy for us in our weakness (Hebrews 4:15).
2. *Treasure the gospel.* Keeping Christ first in your heart and your life (Philippians 3:8) is the foundation for having relationships that last. It's in our nature to bear witness to, and bear the image of, whatever we truly treasure. Let the fragrance of your life and leadership be the aroma of Jesus (2 Corinthians 2:14–15). Your ministry should

stir the desires of others to know of Christ. Confess sin and delight in Christ's forgiveness (James 5:16). The more you personify the gospel, the more you attract friends of grace and grit.

3. *Practice presence.* Technology and social media make parasocial relationships—ones mediated through devices rather than personal presence—seem like the norm. While adding friends on social media may expand your digital imprint, it will neither make you Hopeful nor draw other Hopefuls to you. Hopefuls don't want mediated relationships. Develop life-on-life connections in the context of real community (3 John vv. 13–14).

4. *Anticipate suffering.* Again and again, the Bible reminds us to expect suffering (John 16:33; 1 Peter 4:12). Let suffering season your soul. Become a leader who quickly points to the providence behind pain (Genesis 45:8). Becoming Hopeful means you are not surprised by suffering. You know that suffering includes not only what's happened, but the disorientation and questions that often accompany it. Leaders learn that God is present even when he feels absent. Trusting him when you can't trace his hand forges a durable soul, one that draws leaders and keeps friends.

5. *Pair honesty with empathy.* Our world is used to resonating with pain and expressing sorrow over our suffering. Not a bad thing at all. But for many people, it's the only tool in their belt because they have recused themselves from being surgeons of the soul. Hopefuls call friends to trust God, resist self-pity, press into community, and do hard things. Be a friend who doesn't simply identify with people's pain, but also stirs faith in God's promises and hope for the future (Ephesians 4:15–16).

6. *Respond righteously when you feel sinned against.* A self-righteous or thin-skinned leader will repel potential Hopefuls with their defensiveness and judgment. Temperamental leaders telegraph immaturity. But when a leader exhibits a magnanimous soul who forgives and forbears, others are drawn by their grace and resilience. Hopefuls have received mercy and are eager to pass it along to others (Ephesians 4:32).

7. *Customize your encouragement.* Wise is the leader who recognizes that what animates one may not invigorate another. I have a friend who doesn't need encouraging words about his performance but is touched deeply by gifts. To truly encourage him requires me to think outside my own preferences. Customize your encouragement to

how others are created and motivated. Find what makes people feel valued and use it to help them see God's grace (Hebrews 10:25).

8. *Avoid hasty vulnerability.* Unzipping your full story, complete with all the details of all your brokenness, may be satisfying in the moment, but it can convey emotional immaturity (Proverbs 29:11). Hopefuls are drawn to mature leadership. So, becoming Hopeful means sharing proportionate vulnerability. Few leaders live with shame over saying less up front. Many regret frontloading the relational train with more freight than a new friendship can tow.

9. *Don't keep a tally of who cares more.* Becoming Hopeful is first an exercise of allowing acts of love to expand your soul(1 Corinthians 13:4–5). As love turns us away from our self-obsessions and we bear the pain of others, our souls enlarge. We become more like Christ.

10. *Cultivate compassionate courage.* Follow through with care after a hard conversation (Ephesians 4:15). When someone feels cut by your correction, the salve of your sympathy conveys the sincerity of your love. And it reveals your character too. A true Hopeful draws convictional friends by seasoning convictions with care.

I believe that Bunyan wrote in Hopeful at the river crossing because he wanted to inspire wonder in us. He wanted to encourage his readers to both *be* Hopeful and to *want* Hopeful. By that stage in his life, Bunyan's suffering had taught him much. Isolation and loneliness became his companions for long periods of his ministry journey. I believe his imprisonment and being away from his family convinced him that leaders should not journey alone. We must run together to finish well.

THE RISEN HOPEFUL IS GREATER THAN OUR DOUBTS

There is another Hopeful in our story who is the true hero. We have a greater Hopeful in *Christ*. Because of his astonishing love, substitutionary death, and triumphant resurrection, you—the cracked clay pot—*will* finish well. At the center of God's conspiracy is an unstoppable Savior "who is able to keep you from stumbling and to present you blameless before the presence of his glory with great joy" (Jude v. 24).

Maybe you can relate to Christian right now, struggling along the pastoral path, unable to feel the ground. It's been a bad month, a hard season. Ministry feels barren. Or maybe unexpected suffering has left you with more doubts than you can possibly manage. You stare in the mirror each morning with a different kind of wonder: *I wonder what I'm supposed to do!* The whole journey feels under threat. Your shame is now uncaged. *This was never supposed to be me. I feel like such a hypocrite.*

I've lost count of the number of times I have doubted the goodness of God through this journey. Or his love for me. Or whether he cares, or if my prayers really matter. When pastors are honest, we look a lot less like poster kids for faith and more like the desperate dad who said to Jesus, "I believe; help my unbelief!" (Mark 9:24).

Can you relate? Do you wonder how God feels about you right now? His thoughts are not your thoughts. When God sees you, he is moved with grace and mercy. He's not up in heaven getting angry over your struggles. God doesn't roll his eyes because you are perplexed. His love for you is steadfast and abounding. Yes, you—the doubting pastor, the struggling ministry leader. God has an unquenchable, unrelenting affection for you. Christ has already satisfied God's wrath for all the ways our faith falls short. When God sees you, he is moved with grace and mercy.

Remember when Thomas expressed doubts over Christ's resurrection? Jesus did not retaliate or turn his back on him. He didn't separate him from the other disciples. No, Jesus moved toward him. He engaged him, spoke to his doubts, drew him forward and upward. Jesus was gracious and merciful, abounding in love.

Remember, only one person ever walked the earth with complete confidence in God's promises and a perfect finish to life. It was the Greater Hopeful, Jesus. The rest of us cracked clay pots stumble through a fallen world with decaying bodies, declining minds, and our share of doubting.

Like Christian, you may be far into your journey and doubting your resilience, wondering whether you will make it. But Christ's heart never falters. His love is steadfast. Even when our love loses focus and our feet lose traction, his love still sticks.

Sure you have doubts. So do I. But God's love is greater than our doubts. And he loves us with a perpetual, undying, everlasting love. He is praying fervently for us, and he will not rest until we are free. "Consequently, he is able to save to the uttermost those who draw near to God through him, since he always lives to make intercession for them" (Hebrews 7:25).

Free, finished well, and forever home. It's how your story ends. Mine too. Maybe we both need to contemplate the meaning of that right now. "We are on our way home, and home will be glorious," says J. I. Packer. "And contemplating that glory, however inadequately we do it, will brace minds and hearts to resist the weakening effect, the down-drag into apathy and despair, that pain, hostility, discouragement, isolation, contempt, and being misunderstood—and all the rest of the suffering—might naturally have on us otherwise."[11]

Brace your mind and open wide your imagination. We will stand together on a distant shore realizing God's seven wonders are truly wonderful. They forged a durable life. We suffered, but we trusted. We made it safely across the river. God's conspiracy is now complete. And we will pass through the gates of the Celestial City.

Whole. Happy. And finally *home*.

IT'S WORTH THE FIGHT!

Becoming Hopeful, and journeying with Hopeful, is worth it. I suspect you know this. Deep down, you believe it. This vision syncs with something you long for as you lead.

If you think over your ministry, the moments you most cherish are times where you experienced the wonders of gospel camaraderie. Maybe it was personal when someone helped you see your gifts in a new way. Maybe it was missional, when you united to plant a church, feed the poor, or help another believer break through some constraint.

God made us relational, and he made ministry a shared endeavor. When we unite together in this dangerous journey to glorify God, we are actually being used in the service of a higher purpose. Becoming Hopeful has eternal value and irreplaceable satisfaction. Having Jesus and other Hopefuls with us points to a life well lived.

Certainly, there will be costs. Sometimes potential Hopefuls actually turn out to be Judas or Demas. There will be disappointments along the way. Love is costly. Yet we know that the true wonder lies not in the isolated genius who lives large and dies alone. No. It's Christian, Hopeful, me, you—the average leaders who need help and who help others to finish well.

Together, we are stronger. Together, we get the crown. Together, we become Hopeful. And eventually we will be with Jesus in the glorious Celestial City with no more pain, sorrow, or tears. And there we will behold "an eternal weight of glory beyond all comparison"; not from broken clay pots, but from imperishable and immortal bodies (2 Corinthians 4:17). The mystery of your burdens will be revealed. The conspiracy will be complete. And we will all behold God's plan with wonder, knowing without a shred of doubt, it was all worth it.

QUESTIONS FOR REFLECTION

1. Do you have any Hopefuls in your life? Make a list of the qualities you admire. Be as specific as possible.
2. Remembering that we attract what we embody, what are some areas of growth in your own journey to becoming Hopeful?
3. What does it mean to you to finish well? How might meditating on crossing the River of Death to the Celestial City help you as you face your current struggles?

EPILOGUE

The most exhilarating part of my life right now is raising a four-year-old. And yes, as you might imagine, it's also the hardest thing.

But there is one treasure in this unexpected season that we find irreplaceable: the constant sense of wonder that captures my grandson's imagination. Mountains, fireflies, stars, stories, pictures, the stuff of boyhood—his little soul stands in awe over the enchantments of this world. For him, wonders are just another day-in-the-life of a curious preschooler. For us, each one becomes a fresh opportunity to see creation through his eyes, to look at the world through his wonder.

Somehow, deep within us, God is using his wonder to turn a pilot light into an inferno of desire to fight on and finish well. For I am old enough to know that the world's little wonders signify a greater Wonder that affixes a resurrection to every crucifixion. Smaller wonders escort us toward the more remarkable marvel of how God magnifies his name through weak leaders in a broken world.

I pray the day will come when my grandson connects these earthly wonders to the Eternal One. Because as we have learned in our journey through this book, God's expands our ability and capacity for perseverance as we see and understand the clay pot conspiracy. I want that for him. But I pray for something else too. No matter how flat or democratized the world becomes, leaders will always influence the trajectories of souls and states. My prayer is that our little guy would find himself irresistibly drawn toward leaders that embody the conspiracy. Maybe he, too, will become that kind of leader. Maybe that kind of leader will be you.

Until then, I will watch him marvel over creation while I enjoy the greater Wonder. Sure, my body grows weaker; signals are wheezing now as they cross the synapses in my brain. But I can trust God for what is needed to raise a kid through my sixties (and hopefully beyond). In fact, I can live confident that this assignment is a means of grace to achieve my endurance and

EPILOGUE

sustain my resilience. Why? Because God's power is made perfect in my weakness (2 Corinthians 12:9):

<u>My Weakness</u> + God's Power = Resilience

It's the clay pot conspiracy. The wonder that delivers us home.

ACKNOWLEDGMENTS

Recently I read that a writer's "decline" begins between the ages of forty to fifty-five. There were too many days I felt that reality. But in my post-fifty-five-world, I'm grateful for a community of gifted people bringing a vision to keep my writing alive.

Writing is the marriage of good words and great spaces. The reader can judge whether the words are good. But Brian and Ruth Cassidy and Tony and Summer Yacovetti provided exquisite spaces in which to write. Thank you. Special thanks to Rush Witt, for his persistently pastoral pursuit of this partnership with New Growth Press. I'm finishing the project very grateful for my experience with them. Thanks to Andrew Ballard who ably assisted with edits on several chapters. Barbara Juliani turned her tenured eye toward the larger edits and upgraded every chapter. To the several friends I consulted for counsel on how to approach certain portions of the book, thank you.

And Kimm, who is always the voice that rallies my faith to keep going and makes life so enjoyable when I rest. Lastly, I thank God for helping me to see, then savor, his clay pot conspiracy.

ENDNOTES

Wonder #1

1. Murray J. Harris, *The Second Epistle to the Corinthians: A Commentary on the Greek Text* (William B. Eerdman's Publishing, 2005), 73.

2. Mark A. Seifrid, *The Second Letter to the Corinthians* in *The Pillar New Testament Commentary Series* (PNTC), ed. D. A. Carson (William B. Eerdmans, 2014), 199.

3. Ideas from this chapter were originally presented in a condensed form in my article "The Clay-Pot Conspiracy: Hope for Leaders Losing Heart," for Desiring God, February 27, 2023, https://www.desiringgod.org/articles/the-clay-pot-conspiracy.

4. J. I. Packer, *Weakness Is the Way: Life with Christ Our Strength* (Crossway, 2013), 13.

5. D. A. Carson, *A Model of Christian Maturity* (Baker Books, 1984), 154.

6. Thomas Kidd, "When Our Heroes Don't Live Up to Their Theology," The Gospel Coalition, January 17, 2018, https://www.thegospelcoalition.org/article/when-heroes-dont-live-up-to-their-theology/.

7. Arnold A. Dallimore, *George Whitefield: God's Anointed Servant in the Great Revival of the Eighteenth Century* (Crossway, 1990), 101.

Wonder #2

1. Paul Miller, *The J Curve: Dying and Rising with Jesus in Everyday Life* (Crossway, 2019), 68.

2. Sam Storms, *A Sincere and Pure Devotion to Christ: 100 Daily Meditations on 2 Corinthians* (Volume, 2 Corinthians 1–6) (Crossway, 2010), 3.

3. Carl R. Trueman, *Reformation: Yesterday, Today, and Tomorrow* (Christian Focus, 2000), 48–49.

Wonder #3

1. Thomas Watson, *Heaven Taken by Storm* (Monergism Books, 2019), 35.

2. Barbara Duguid, *Extravagant Grace: God's Glory Displayed in Our Weakness* (P&R Publishing, 2013), 81.

3. In the first two chapters of *I Still Do* (Baker Books, 2020), I write more extensively on how acknowledging sin as our biggest problem doesn't mean sin is the only problem. Human brokenness is broader than sin.

4. Elisabeth Elliot, *Loneliness: It Can Be a Wilderness, It Can Be a Pathway* (Thomas Nelson, 1988), 53.

5. J. I. Packer, *Taking Repentance Seriously* (Anglican Network in Canada, 2007), 7.

Wonder #4

1. J. R. R. Tolkien, *The Hobbit* (Mariner Books, 2012), 6.

2. Gavin Ortlund, *Humility: The Joy of Self-Forgetfulness* (Crossway, 2022).

3. PatrickRsGhost, "People who have owned sheep," Reddit, August 31, 2018, https://www.reddit.com/r/AskReddit/comments/9c0265/comment/e574nbg/.

4. During this period, the family of churches was more of a network. Becoming a denomination came later.

5. J. Oswald Sanders, *Spiritual Leadership* (Moody Press, 1989), 142.

6. David Brooks, *The Road to Character* (Random House, 2015), 196.

7. Andy Crouch, *Playing God: Redeeming the Gift of Power* (InterVarsity Press, 2013), 219–20.

8. C. S. Lewis, *The Screwtape Letters* (Harper Collins, 2001), 7.

9. William Cowper, "God Moves in a Mysterious Way," (1774), *The Book of Hymns: A Fresh Anthology of Favorite Hymns* (Wordsworth Reference, 2007), 7.

Wonder #5

1. William Cowper, "Welcome Cross," (1779), Olney Hymn #35, https://allpoetry.com/Olney-Hymn-35:-Welcome-Cross.

Wonder #6

1. Zach Eswine, *The Imperfect Pastor: Discovering Joy in Our Limitations Through a Daily Apprenticeship with Jesus* (Crossway, 2015), 26.

2. Paul Miller, *The J Curve: Dying and Rising with Jesus in Everyday Life* (Crossway, 2019), 294.

3. Arnold Dallimore, *George Whitefield* (Banner of Truth Trust, 1980), 514.

4. Sam Crabtree, *Practicing Affirmation: God-Centered Praise of Those Who Are Not* God (Crossway, 2011), 12.

5. If you would like further study on how elderships influence church culture, I've written a book titled, *The Plurality Principle: How to Build and Maintain a Thriving Church Leadership Team*. The book extrapolates one central idea to help churches flourish: The quality of the plurality determines the health of the church.

6. Arthur C. Brooks, *From Strength to Strength: Finding Success, Happiness, and Deep Purpose in the Second Half of Life* (Portfolio/Penguin, 2022), 177.

7. John Piper, *A Hunger for God: Desiring God through Fasting and Prayer* (Crossway, 2013), 99.

8. J. D. Greear, *Gaining by Losing: Why the Future Belongs to Churches That Send* (Zondervan, 2015), 45.

9. Jonathan Leeman, "How Mark Dever Passes Out Authority," The Gospel Coalition, January 16, 2014, https://www.thegospel coalition.org/article/how-mark-dever-passes-out-authority/.

Wonder #7

1. John Bunyan, *Grace Abounding to the Chief of Sinners* in *The Works of John Bunyan*, ed. George Offor, vol. 1, *Experimental, Doctrinal, and Practical* (W. G. Blackie and Sons, 1854; repr. Banner of Truth Trust, 1991), 23.

2. Jacob Tanner, *The Tinker's Progress: The Life and Times of John Bunyan* (Christian Focus Publications, 2024), 167.

3. Edmund Venables, *The Life of John Bunyan* (Transcribed from the 1888 Walter Scott Edition by David Price), Kindle Edition, chapter 9.

4. John Bunyan, *The Pilgrim's Progress* (B&H Publishing Group, 2017), 226.

5. William Revell Moody, *The Life of Dwight L. Moody* (Fleming H. Revell, 1900), 552.

6. Bunyan, *Pilgrim's Progress*, x (preface).

7. Bunyan, *Pilgrim's Progress*, 228.

8. Charles H. Spurgeon, "An Instructive Truth" (Sermon #2893). Delivered on Thursday Evening, June 22, 1876, at the Metropolitan Tabernacle and published on Thursday, July 21, 1904.

9. Richard Baxter, *A Christian Directory*, quoted in J. I. Packer, *A Quest for Godliness* (Crossway, 1990), 262.

10. J. R. R. Tolkien, *The Lord of the Rings* (HarperCollins, 1991), 919.

11. J. I. Packer, *Weakness Is the Way: Life with Christ Our Strength* (Crossway, 2013), 102.